T0384265

Adolescents, Family and Consumer Behaviour

Buying decision making is a complicated process, in which a consumer's decision is under the influence of others. The buyer's decision making is directed in such a way that they must act as a consumer in society. Media and family are key socializing agents for adolescents. Moreover, changes in the socio-cultural environment in India necessitate that adolescents' influence in family's buying decision making should be investigated. In comparison to Western society, Indian society is quite different when compared in terms of family composition and structure, behavior, values and norms which impact adolescents' buying decision making.

Adolescents, Family and Consumer Behaviour studies the role of consumer socialization agents for adolescents, examining socio-economic factors that influence adolescents' buying decision making in Indian urban families. It aims to discover the influence tactics that adolescents employ and to qualitatively analyse how marketers in turn influence adolescents. It addresses the topics with regard to strategic management and marketing and will be of interest to researchers, academics, practitioners, and students in the fields of management, entrepreneurship, small business management, and human resource management.

Dr Harleen Kaur has served as Assistant Professor of Management at Asra Institute of Advanced Studies, Bhawanigarh, Punjab, India since 2013. She completed her PhD in 2019 at Punjabi University, Patiala. She finished her MBA in HR at RIMT, Mandi Gobindgarh in 2011. She has published around 15 papers in various international journals and conference proceedings. She has published around 16 books. Previously, she served as HR (Executive) at International Farm Fresh Products (India), Ltd, Channo (Bhawanigarh), Punjab, India from 2011 to 2013. Her main research areas are HR, marketing, adolescents' and family buying decision making. She has worked on software, PSAW, MS-Excel (for AHP, TOPSIS, VIKOR) and MS-Office.

Dr Chandan Deep Singh has been serving as an assistant professor in the Department of Mechanical Engineering at Punjabi University, Patiala, Punjab, India since 2011. He completed his PhD in November 2016 at the same institution. His Master's of technology in manufacturing systems engineering is from the Sant Longowal Institute of Engineering and Technology in Longowal, Sangrur, Punjab, India, completed in 2011. He was awarded his Bachelor's of technology in mechanical engineering in 2009 from Giani Zail Singh College of Engineering and Technology in Bathinda, Punjab, India. He has published around 53 books and guided 55 students in their Master's of technology thesis. He has published around 100 papers in various international journals and conference proceedings. Presently, eight students are working under him for their PhD, and one for his Master's of technology. His main research areas are CAD/CAM, production and industrial engineering, and die-casting. He has worked on software, namely CATIA, ProE, Solid Works, PSAW, MS-Excel (for AHP, TOPSIS, VIKOR), AMOS (in PSAW for SEM) and MATLAB.

Routledge Focus on Business and Management

The fields of business and management have grown exponentially as areas of research and education. This growth presents challenges for readers trying to keep up with the latest important insights. Routledge Focus on Business and Management presents small books on big topics and how they intersect with the world of business research.

Individually, each title in the series provides coverage of a key academic topic, whilst collectively, the series forms a comprehensive collection across the business disciplines.

Employment Relations and Ethnic Minority Enterprise
An Ethnography of Chinese Restaurants in the UK
Xisi Li

Women, Work and Migration
Nursing in Australia
Diane van den Broek and Dimitria Groutsis

Distributed Leadership and Digital Innovation
The Argument for Couple Leadership
Caterina Maniscalco

Public Relations Crisis Communication
A New Model
Lisa Anderson-Meli and Swapna Koshy

Adolescents, Family and Consumer Behaviour
A Behavioural Study of Adolescents in Indian Urban Families
Dr Harleen Kaur and Dr Chandan Deep Singh

For more information about this series, please visit: www.routledge.com/ Routledge-Focus-on-Business-and-Management/book-series/FBM

Adolescents, Family and Consumer Behaviour

A Behavioural Study of Adolescents in Indian Urban Families

Dr Harleen Kaur and
Dr Chandan Deep Singh

Routledge
Taylor & Francis Group

NEW YORK AND LONDON

First published 2020
by Routledge
52 Vanderbilt Avenue, New York, NY 10017

and by Routledge
2 Park Square, Milton Park, Abingdon, Oxon OX14 4RN

Routledge is an imprint of the Taylor & Francis Group, an informa business

British Library Cataloguing-in-Publication Data
A catalogue record for this book is available from the British Library

Library of Congress Cataloging-in-Publication Data
Names: Kaur, Harleen (Professor of management), author. | Singh,
Chandan Deep, author.
Title: Adolescents, family and consumer behaviour : a behavioural
study of adolescents in Indian urban families / Dr Harleen Kaur
and Dr Chandan Deep Singh.
Description: New York, NY : Routledge, 2019 | Series: Routledge
focus on business & management | Includes bibliographical
references and index.
Identifiers: LCCN 2019049358 | ISBN 9780367408893 (hbk) |
ISBN 9780367810276 (ebk)
Subjects: LCSH: Young consumers–India. | Teenage consumers–
India. | Families–Decision making–India.
Classification: LCC HC440.C6 K38 2019 | DDC
658.8/34208350954–dc23

LC record available at https://lccn.loc.gov/2019049358

ISBN: 978-0-367-40889-3 (hbk)
ISBN: 978-0-367-81027-6 (ebk)

Typeset in Times New Roman
by Wearset Ltd, Boldon, Tyne and Wear

Contents

Figures

Tables

Equations

Abbreviations

AHP	Analytical Hierarchical Process
ANOVA	Analysis of Variance
CFA	Confirmatory Factor Analysis
CI	Consistency Index
CR	Consistency Ratio
EFA	Exploratory Factor Analysis
FA	Factor Analysis
FSM	Flexible Systems Methodology
MCDM	Multiple Criteria Decision Making
NIS	Negative Ideal Solution
PAF	Principal Axis Factoring
PASW	Predictive Analytics Software
PCA	Principal Component Analysis
PIS	Positive Ideal Solution
PPS	Percent Point Score
RI	Random Index
SMS	Short Message Service
SMTU	Screen Media Time Usage
SPSS	Statistical Package for Social Sciences
TOPSIS	Technique for Order Preference by Similarity to Ideal Solution
VIKOR	Vlse Kriterijumska Optimizacija I KOmpromisno Resenje
WHO	World Health Organization

1 Introduction

Socialization is a psychological process that determines the behaviour of a person. It has been described as the process by which individuals are able to acquire knowledge, dispositions and skills, thus enabling them to participate in groups and the society (Brim, 1966). In past research, Ward (1974) investigated the customer behaviour of young people through the conceptual framework of socialization. As per John (1999), the research on behaviour of adolescents prospered in the 1970s, although researchers have been interested in it from 1950. In 1974, Ward highlighted the need for socialization of adolescents into the customer role. Customer socialization is the process in which an adolescent learns knowledge, values and skills related to customer behaviour due to interaction with socialization agents such as parents, media, school and fellows (Shim and Gehrt, 1996). Ward (1974) defined customer socialization as "the process by which young people acquire knowledge, values and skills necessary for their functioning as customers in the marketplace".

Zigler and Child (1969) described it as a broad term for the whole process by which an individual is able to develop his or her patterns of socially relevant behaviours and experience. It is an indefinite process that assumes that an individual changes his or her behaviour continuously. In other words, it is the process which describes the way in which an individual learns how to behave in society according to his or her position.

John (1999) described the adolescents' stage as the reflective stage because in this the knowledge of market concepts becomes more expressive. During this stage, strategic decision making is adopted by adolescents. Buying decision making is a complicated process, in which a customer's decision is under the impact of others. The buying decision making is directed in a way that they have to act as customers in society. Media and family are key socialising agents for adolescents. Moreover, changes in the socio-cultural environment in India necessitate that adolescents' influence in a family's buying decision making should be investigated. In comparison to

Western society, Indian society is quite different, when compared in terms of family composition and structure, behaviour, values and norms which effect adolescents' buying decision making. Hence, this work aims not only in exploring the research already carried out by earlier researchers in Western countries as well as India but also in identifying recommendations for future research.

The World Health Organization (WHO) defines adolescence as "the phase in human growth and development which occurs after the childhood and before adulthood, from ages 10 to 19" (www.who.int/maternal_adolescent_adolescent/topic/adolescence/dev/en). "Customer Socialisation of Adolescents" is a practice which helps adolescents in learning to become customers. Adolescence is a period in life when young people learn different roles in society. Being a "customer" is one such role. During adolescence, young people start purchasing independently (McNeal and Yeh, 1997). Adolescence is very closely associated with possessing customer goods as adolescents in today's world need products for expressing their social identity (Lueg and Ponder, 2006).

Adolescents are an important segment of the market. India has the largest potential customer base of adolescents in the whole world as among India's population of 1210.19 million at the end of 2011 (Census of India, 2011), 362.87 million (31.1%) are under the age of 14 (Chaudhary and Gupta, 2014). It is believed that preferences and attitude developed during the adolescent age are carried over into adulthood (Hurlock, 1968).

The merchandiser faces difficulty in determining an appropriate strategy, in order to counter the customers' behaviour changes. This study attempts to find out the role of adolescents in buying decision making as there is a radical change in the buying behaviour of adolescents due to urbanization, as it leads to change in product marketing strategies. India has just started to witness the change and coping with it is the need of the hour.

Parental employment status also has an impact on adolescents' buying decision making. If parents are working, adolescents are given more freedom for their choices and spending. Parents provide autonomy, support their views and opinions and restrict them, if needed. Each family member plays a different role in decision making within the family. They may initiate demand for any product or service, may decide on what to buy, from where to buy, how to pay for products and services, ways to consume them and benefits expected from such products and services and sharing their roles in maintaining the products and services. The role of mother and father varies in the family. Adolescents play a significant role in a family's buying decision making for their own as well as products for other members of the family.

Adolescents vocalize their wishes, and parents are often co-operative and attentive. Parents understand that adolescents influence what is bought but it was also found that they do not agree on the influence adolescents have. Thus, there is a gap in the knowledge about what is happening that seemingly cannot be solved through retrospective data collection. In our society, being patriarchal, adolescents play an important role in buying decisions in the family, which may be due to the sociological changes taking place. Parents have the decisive vote, but in this "decisive vote" they take adolescents' views and prior experiences with them into account.

In present times, we see a drastic change, where adolescents are now viewed as customers for every type of product. Adolescents are now treated as a segment in the market which cannot be ignored. They are considered a primary market of customers, who have their own money for their own needs and direct the use of their parents' money for their benefit, and a future market for all the goods and services will provide a steady stream of new customers when they reach the market. Thus, when considering these, marketers have understood the potential of this segment and, thus, have started targeting it.

With increasing competition and a changing social and economic environment, it is essential for the marketers to be customer-oriented. The buying behaviour of customers plays an important role in marketing planning. The awareness of customer behaviour has presented new dimensions in marketing practices. It is important for every business enterprise to know its customers and their buying behaviour. As culture influences a family unit, it is quite likely that socialization of adolescents is influenced by these.

Adolescents, while buying, impose their demands on parents because they have many sources of information along with greater exposure. Somewhat they succeed in pressurizing their parents for desired products as parents value their views and nurture their self-expression but, on the other hand, some demographic factors minimize this influence. With dual income (both mother and father having a good income), the purchasing power of a family increases and a psychological aspect gets attached to it. Due to these, every message targeting the adults must be reframed. Marketers should consider the ways for capturing the attention of two different audiences in a single message. They must appeal to the adults, as well as to the adolescents who influence them. Adolescents neither think nor buy like adults but influence their parents' purchases of everything.

The role that adolescents play in decision making concerning the whole family has prompted researchers to pay attention to the study of influence of adolescents. Adolescents' influence varies by product category and stage of the decision-making process. For some products, they are buyers, information seekers and active initiators; whereas for other products, they influence buying decision making of parents. Buying decision making is governed by how they have been socialized to act as customers. Family members, media and peers are key socializing agents for them

1.1 Changing Adolescence in Society

Adolescence in social study is the living phase in an individual's life for physical and mental development. Through improvements in education and care for them, there is a rising influence of adolescents in society.

In present times' interfamilial decision making, communication in the family has become more modern, open and democratic: the changing structure of the family and working women have had a reflective influence on the growing economic power, control and independence of adolescents, with the result that they are now taking charge and influencing their family's decision-making process more than they did in the previous generation (Kaur and Medury, 2011). Adolescents' lifestyle has changed a lot in comparison to the previous generation, as in today's world, they are fed by mobiles, tablets, television (TV) and other media, which cause them to have an isolated world of their own fantasy.

Adolescents are forced to enter the grown-up world earlier than they should. This has led them to decide their own wants and needs. They prefer to "think for themselves" than to obey their parents. On the other hand, a mother's presence in the workplace also supports the practice and legitimates adolescents as customers. A previous study indicated that increases in maternal employment cause changes in the desired qualities of adolescents. They have more responsibilities when their mothers are employed. This could lead to increased maturity and sense of self-reliance (Adib and El-Bassiouny, 2012). They remain a significant customer group that food manufacturers cannot neglect to overlook. They are a market force that should be recognized and ideally satisfied. They have specific demands when it comes to food and drink that require a unique approach to marketing and product development. Each year, in America, the purchase influence of adolescents increases with age.

Because the current generation of young customers makes more decisions than previous generations, they influence more family decisions, especially in terms of food buying. The role that adolescents play in influencing the family's decisions has attracted researchers to analyse them. The adolescents' market needs special kinds of marketing techniques to be utilized in order to explore their thought process and gain better understanding. They constitute three different markets: the current target market, the future target market and the influential.

1.2 Role of Adolescents in Buying Decision Making

Understanding customers' behaviour is most important to merchandisers so that they can develop effective strategies. Although the end result is to sell a product, which is considered most important, it is equally important to understand what is in the minds of the customers before they buy the product. In a basic unit of a family, the numbers and members vary from family to family, and so there is a lot of saying that goes into the buying decision making, which many times is unknown and unseen to the marketer.

Members in a family influence the decision-making process for different products and to varying degrees, based on the kind of product and the way they intend to use the product. Thus, the marketer should not just target individual family members, but rather the family as a whole. Studies show that out of all the family members, adolescents have started to emerge as a growing influence on family buying decision making in a variety of product ranges – not just products meant for them, but also those used by the entire family. Gone are the days when marketers would solely focus on the adults as targets to market their products. Adolescents then were not considered an important section of the market that needed to be focused on.

In the twenty-first century, adolescents are viewed as customers for every type of product – be it a household or a luxury item. They are now considered an important segment in the market that marketers cannot afford to ignore. Thus, when considering that adolescents spend their own money for their own needs and wants and influence parents' buying decision making and are a steady stream of future customers, marketers understood the potential of this huge segment and thus have started targeting this segment.

In the context of increasing competition and the changing economic and social environment, it becomes essential for the marketers to be agile. Customers' buying decision making plays a significant role in strategic marketing planning. The recent awareness of customer behaviour has introduced many new dimensions into marketing philosophy and practices. It is both relevant and important for every business enterprise to know its customers and understand their buying behaviour. "Family as a consuming and decision making unit is a central phenomenon in marketing and customer behaviour" (Ahluwalia and Sanan, 2016). Family always plays a very important mediating function. It combines the individual with larger society, where the person learns various roles suitable for an adult life (Achenreiner, 1977). Since culture exerts considerable influence on the family unit, it is also likely that cultural variables influence the socialization process of the adolescents.

Adolescents in India have become the most important object of research. India has one of the largest populations of adolescents in the world, and Indian adolescents have substantial economic power and unique influence on their parents. Research indicates that adolescents play a significant role in some family buying decisions, and their influence varies by product categories and decisional stages (Moschis and Moore, 1979). In general, for products in which the adolescent is directly involved in consumption, the adolescent is expected to have at least some influence on the decision.

1.2.1 Buying Roles

Buying decision making is composed of a sequence of decisions, and different family members may play different roles at different stages (Alsmadi and Khizindar, 2015). In general, the roles are likely to vary between families, with demographic variables, different product types, time and even individual decisions. This variation can be observed both within a single role and across roles. "Influence is inferred when one person acts in such a way as to change the behaviour of another in some intended manner" (Bergadaà, 2007). Thus adolescents' influence is characterized by actions that make a difference during one or more of the family decision stages. An influencer in a family does not necessarily have expertise, and he/she can influence one or more of the decision-making stages in varying roles and with varying impacts.

Various buying roles are:

1   **Initiator:** A person who first suggests the idea of buying the particular product or service.
2   **Influencer:** A person whose view or advice influences the decision.
3   **Decider:** A person who decides on any component of a buying decision; whether to buy, what to buy, how to buy or where to buy
4   **Buyer:** The person who makes the actual purchase.
5   **User:** A person who consumes or uses the product or service.

A company needs to identify these roles because they have implications for designing the product, determining messages and allocating the promotional budget. If the husband decides on the car make then the auto company will direct advertising to reach husbands. The auto company might design certain car features to please the wife. Knowing the main participants and their roles helps the marketer fine-tune the marketing programme. Consider the selection of a family automobile. The teenage son may have suggested buying a new car. A friend might advise the family on the kind of car to buy. The husband might choose the make. The wife might have definite desires regarding the car's size and interior. The husband might make the financial offer. The wife might use the car more often than her husband. Another example of the same: a kindergarten girl needs to buy colour crayons to use in class. (1) Initiator: the girl; (2) Influencer: her teacher or her classmates; (3) Decider: either of the parents; (4) Buyer: either of the parents or a sibling; (5) User: the girl herself.

The degree of influence exerted by adolescents depends on how interested or involved they are in the product or purchase. Products for their own use are likely to be perceived as the most personally relevant. Hence the adolescent is expected to have the strongest influence on decisions for products which they are directly involved in consuming. In contrast, they are expected to have significantly less influence when purchases are not for self-use or have low relevance for them; they may not be motivated to influence these decisions, and thereby a moderate influence is assumed.

Adolescents' influence is also expected to be lower for family products that involve substantial financial outlays such as TVs and cars. Due to the financial risk associated with these family products, parents will more likely prefer to make these decisions without permitting the adolescent to influence them to any appreciable degree. Moreover adolescents are thus assumed to have least influence on durable and expensive products.

Parents prefer to do the more instrumental activities for themselves; roles that involve doing the tasks that affect the final buying decision, such as the timing of a purchase, location of a purchase or determining the amount spent. On the other hand, parents allow adolescents to have increasing influence on the more expressive sub-decisions, e.g. product attributes such as colour, model and brand choices (Belch *et al.*, 2005). One reason for adolescents' lower influence relative to their parents' in later stages of the decision process may be that adolescents lack the experience necessary to make informed decisions for instrumental activities. Another reason could be that parents have greater financial investments in most durable purchases (Burgess and Steenkamp, 2006). So parents will exert power where it counts – in the actual decision.

The family has been identified as the most important decision-making and consumption unit (Chan, 2013). Family decision making is considered more complex than individual decision making because it includes different participants with different choices and roles. Adolescents' product-related knowledge and information were viewed positively and encouraged by parents. According to (Chaplin and John, 2007), an influencer in a family does not necessarily have expertise, and he/she can influence one or more of the decision-making stages in varying roles and with varying impacts. Influences are distributed in two types: first, based on decision stages (idea generation, choice of alternatives, etc.) and, second, based on decision areas (type, brand, price and shop). Family constitutes a bundle of customers which consists of different needs and wants regarding purchasing. Consequently buying decisions are also made on considering these diversities found among the members. Among these customers some younger customers make their presence felt in buying decisions.

Some adolescents succeed in pressurizing their parents to buy desired products because parents approve their autonomy and nurture their self-expression and value their views but, on the other hand, there are some demographic factors which minimize this influence. Demands made by young children are not always fulfilled but still many of their demands are converted into buying. This tendency depends on various aspects like age, family income, gender of adolescent etc. As dual income increases the purchasing power of the family, a psychological aspect becomes attached to it, described below.

Today, females are in search of lucrative careers in order to get a sound financial backup. Financial independence is something to which every female aspires. This makes them independent and able to make their own life decisions . Planning of a career or rather a stable career has resulted into late marriages which has further relayed into delayed parenthood. This delayed parenthood can make parents over-emotional towards their young children. Increased income enables parents to splurge on young children to make them glad. Due to working parents, families have been divided into nuclear and single parent families in India apart from joint families. Adolescents exert more influence in single parent and nuclear families. As family size increased influence also increased. Adolescents get more options for fulfilling their demands in joint families and absence of parents makes them more powerful.

Parents' employment status also differentiates the impact of adolescents on buying decisions. If parents are working adolescents get more freedom to discuss their choices and spending. Parents provide consumption autonomy, support their views and opinions and put in restrictions if needed. In this way they try to compensate for their unavailability for their adolescent. Most of studies focused on the mother–adolescent relationship and very few on father–adolescent. Studies revealed that adolescents spend their most of the time with their mothers so mothers are not persuaded to buy by the adolescents, while mostly it is easy for adolescents to convince their fathers.

Family members play different roles in making decisions within the family. They may initiate demand for products and services, may decide on which brand to buy, where to buy, how to pay for products and services, how to consume them, what benefits to expect from such products and services and how to share their roles in maintaining the products and services. The roles of father and mother may vary in the family depending upon the role played by them in their families. Adolescents are very important role in family buying decision making for their own products as well as products used or consumed by other family members.

It was found that for TV, the demand was initiated and influenced mostly by adolescents but for refrigerators and washing machines, it was done mostly by females. It was revealed that although the demand was initiated and influenced mostly by adolescents and female members of the family, the final decision and payment was done mostly by male members. This indicates that even today our society is a patriarchal one and adolescents are playing an increasingly important role in the buying decision making of the family, which may be attributed to the sociological changes taking place. Parents perceive themselves to have the decisive vote, but in this "decisive vote" parents take adolescents' manifestations and prior experiences with the adolescents into account.

Adolescents do have significant impacts in various ways through a broad array of techniques, directly and indirectly, consciously and unconsciously. Adolescents vocalize their wishes, and parents are often attentive and co-operative. Parents know that their adolescents influence what they buy in supermarkets but it was also found that parents and adolescents do not agree on just how much influence adolescents have. Thus, a gap exists in the knowledge about what is actually happening in this grey zone of grocery shopping which seemingly cannot be solved through retrospective data collection. Family shopping is neither a completely rational nor conscious process, which makes the use of self-reported behaviour problematic. The adolescents are more influential on need recognition, where to buy, when to buy and which to buy sub-decisions. On the other hand, the parents perceive adolescents to have very little influence on family decision making, as they state themselves as the most influential units of family decision making. The buying intentions may be mediated by parents. Thus parental authority holds significance in buying decision making.

Current changes in social and demographic structures are increasing adolescents' influence on their parents' decisions and their general involvement in family decision making. Higher family income and more women in the workplace have been debated as some of the factors that cause the greater influence of adolescents in the family. As adolescents' role in family decisions increases, research and studies concerning this matter have also become more remarkable and more interesting, especially for marketers and food industries. The previous and recent studies have discussed perceptions from both parents and adolescents; most have merely obtained the data on the amount or type of influence that adolescents applied. Adolescents' influence in family buying decisions has also generally been investigated in a more specific context, focusing mainly on the products that are primarily used by adolescents.

1.3   Customer Socialization of Adolescents

Adolescents influence family purchase decisions as they acquire the basic communication skills needed to interact with other family members. As they grow older they develop more sophisticated buying skills and abilities. They become aware of different socialization agents that convey norms, attitudes, motivations and behaviour to the learner (Jorgensen and Savla, 2010). Much evidence shows that parents, peers, mass media, stores, schools, brands and product themselves and their packages are all sources of information namely socialization agents (Ward, 1974; Dotson and Hyatt, 2005). Adolescents move through various cognitive and social phases in their journey from birth to adolescence and adulthood.

The "socialization of the customer" approach was suggested by (Ward, 1974) as a tool to be used to study customer behaviour. Ward describes the socialization of the customer as a process in which "young people acquire the relevant skills, knowledge and attitudes necessary to act efficiently in the market as customers" (Langrehr and Barry, 1977). The concept of socialization of the customer only includes young people in this description, whereas the scope of the concept today has been broadened to include also the development of relevant cognitions, attitudes and behaviours about consumption in adolescence and adult periods (Ward, 1974).

1.3.1   Socializing Stages

Customer socialization occurs in the perspective of significant cognitive changes and social developments, which take place in a progression of stages as adolescents become socialized into their role as customers. These changes take place as adolescents move through three stages of customer socialization, which are introduced from the perceptual stage (age 3–7) to the analytical stage (age 7–11), then to the reflective stage (age 11–16).

Adolescents in the perceptual stage have limited awareness of information sources, whereas adolescents in the analytical stage have an increased awareness of personal and mass media sources. Adolescents in the reflective stage have contingent use of different information sources depending on the product or situation.

As adolescents grow older, they develop a better knowledge and understanding of different information sources and organize these sources in a

Table 1.1 Customer Socialization Stages

Characteristics	Perceptual Stage (3–7 Years)	Analytical Stage (7–11 Years)	Reflective Stage (11–16 Years)
Knowledge structures: orientation	Concrete representation	Abstract representation	Abstract representation
Focus	Perceptual features	Functional/underlying features	Functional/underlying features
Complexities of knowledge structures	Unidirectional/simple	Two or more dimensions/ contingent ("if–then")	Multidimensional/contingent ("if–then")
Perspective	Egocentric (own perspective)	Dual (own + others) perspective	Dual perspectives in social context
Decision making and influence strategies: orientation	Expedient	Thoughtful	Strategic
Focus (when considering product features	Perceptual/salient features	Functional/underlying/relevant features	Functional/underlying/relevant features

Source: John, 1999.

more flexible way. They also develop preferences for specific information sources. The customer socialization theory helps researchers realize that the age stages of an adolescent are an important factor with regard to the adolescents' influence on family decision making.

1.3.1.1 Perceptual Stage (3–7 Years)

The perceptual stage emphasizes that adolescents' perception is concrete and disparate from abstract or symbolic thought. The perceptual stage is distinguished by a self-orientation upon the immediate and readily observable perceptual features or type of the marketplace. Adolescents' customer knowledge is characterized by perceptual features and differences, often based on a single dimension and represented in concrete details from their own observations. These adolescents reveal familiarity with concepts in the marketplace, such as brands or retail stores, but they understand little about these concepts.

Adolescents in the perceptual stage are still oriented towards themselves, they concentrate only on a single dimension, and they perceive the objects in their environment based on their own perspective: in terms of making the decision or influencing strategies, adolescents during this stage have limited information in helping them make a decision or influencing others with regards to their own perception. The orientations in this stage are simple, practical and self-centred. Decisions are often made on the basis of very limited information, usually a single perceptual dimension. For example, adolescents during this stage can be expected to make their food choice based on a single attribute or dimension, such as the size (small or big).

Adolescents use their egocentric perspective in establishing their influence strategies: they are unable to consider or involve another person's perspectives in modifying their influence strategies or when it comes to negotiating for the desired items. Even though they realize that their parents or friends have other thoughts or perceptions, adolescents during this stage have difficulty thinking about their own perspective and at the same time thinking about other people's perspectives.

1.3.1.2 Analytical Stage (7–11 Years)

At this stage, immense changes occur, both cognitively and socially. This period restrains some of the significant developments in terms of customer knowledge and skills. The change from perceptual thoughts to more symbolic thoughts described by Jean Piaget, along with tremendous increases in information processing abilities, results in a more sophisticated understanding of the marketplace, a more complex set of knowledge about different concepts such as assortment of products and brands, and a new perspective that goes beyond their feelings and motives.

Concepts such as products and prices are analysed and differentiated on the basis of more than one dimension, and generalizations are drawn from one's experience. Reasoning proceeds at a more abstract level, for example adolescents during this stage are able to recognize the motive of the advertiser in trying to sell the products and that sometimes the advertiser does not tell the truth about the product information. There are great changes in analysing the stimuli on multiple dimensions and the acknowledgement of possibilities in adolescents' customer decision-making skills and developing strategies.

Adolescents in the analytical stage demonstrate more thoughtfulness in their choices, considering more than just their own perception, and they are able to utilize a decision strategy that seems to make sense in their environment. Consequently, adolescents are more flexible in the approach they take in making decisions, allowing them to be more adaptive, open and responsive towards their environment's perceptions and thoughts.

1.3.1.3 Reflective Stage (11–16 Years)

The reflective stage is characterized by further progress in several dimensions or aspects of cognitive and social development. Knowledge and familiarity about marketplace concepts such as product assortments, price level or variety of brands become even more complex as adolescents increase more sophisticated information processing and social skills. Adolescents during this stage are able to think in a more reasoning and reflective way. They are able to focus more on the social meanings and underpinnings of the customer marketplace. An increase of awareness towards other people's perception, together with a need to shape their own identity and conform to group expectations, results in more attention to the social aspects of being a customer, making choices and consuming brands. Buying or consuming decisions are made in a more adaptive manner and depend on the situation, condition and task. Influence strategies are considered and planned by adjusting to other people's perspectives, which they think will be better accepted than just a simple approach.

Adolescents from 3 to 7 are in a preoperational stage when cognitive structure is inadequately organized and language skills are developing. In this stage, parents may allow some limited purchase choices – for example concerning the flavours of ice cream or beverages. From 8 to 11 years of age, adolescents are in a concrete operational stage in which they are developing more complex abilities to practise their logical thought to real problems. In this stage, adolescents are starting to develop the persuasive techniques learned from their peers or media to influence their parents to buy what they want. The third phase is when adolescents approach their formal operational stage, from 12 to 15 years old.

Adolescents have greater financial resources and cognitive capabilities to make decisions on a broader range of product categories. Adolescents are able to buy what they want with their own money (adolescents at the reflective stage obtain more pocket money from their parents than younger adolescents). The customer socialization stages together with the Piaget cognitive development phases capture the important changes in how adolescents think, how they perceive others' perceptions and how they articulate themselves as customers in the marketplace. This study focuses on adolescents during their analytical stage (second stage of customer socialization). Adolescents during their analytical stage begin to develop their customer skills and knowledge; therefore it is interesting to analyse how they practise and demonstrate these abilities in their environment.

1.3.2 Socializing Processes

Hypotheses that take socialization of the customer as a model argue that customer behaviour is acquired through interaction between the individual and various socialization agents in certain social environments that are directly or indirectly related to consumption. Within the process of socialization of the customer, the knowledge, norms, beliefs, attitudes and behaviours related to consumption are transferred to the adolescent through specific resources that are also known as socialization agents (Lachance and Legault, 2007). It is possible, by taking into consideration these aspects, to describe the socialization of the adolescent as a customer as:

> the process where the adolescent learns the knowledge, skills, attitudes, values and incentive factors related to consumption behaviours as a result of his/her interaction with socialization agents which include various social institutions and persons such as family, fellows, media and school.
>
> (Shim and Gehrt, 1996)

The learning process undergone by the customer can be studied both as a cognitive and psychological adaptation process and as a social process. Accordingly, an appropriate model could be used. The model introduced includes all levels of the customer socialization process and addresses the major variables influencing the adolescence period (Langrehr, 1979).

1.3.2.1   Individual Factors

Individual factors include elements that are related to the past experiences of the individual and arise from his or her macro surroundings. These include socio-economic level, gender and age.

Socio-economic level. The socio-economic level affects adolescents' preferences for brands and shops. Income distribution and differentiation may result in considerable differences in the purchasing power of the individual. Therefore, the criterion employed by low-income families for evaluation of a good (cheapness, endurance, etc.) is generally different from those of high-income families (quality, elegance, famous brand, etc.). This situation may naturally have a direct influence on the adolescents' learning about being a customer and their acquisition of some of the basic customer skills.

The socio-economic level also affects the adolescents' relationship with family and friends. Adolescents at a high socio-economic level interact more with their families in matters related to consumption and take their family's consumption habits as models. According to the study by Moschis and Moore, 1979, families at high socio-economic levels approach the views of their adolescents with a more modern attitude, allow the adolescents to influence purchasing behaviour of the family and approve of their customer identities. However, friends play an effective role in socialization of adolescents from a low socio-economic level, whereas mass media tools such as newspapers and TV are more effective in socialization of adolescents from higher socio-economic levels (Ozgen, 1995).

Age and life period. Age has been addressed as a major explanatory variable in many studies on the socialization of the customer. Makela and Peters (2004) argued that a large part of socialization develops until the age of 15. Adolescents of 15 years and older possess more information on prices, have strong materialist values and also socially accepted behaviours regarding consumption. Therefore, as they get older, adolescents use more information resources in purchasing, behave more objectively in evaluating goods and better understand marketing practices and policies.

Gender. A close relationship is observed in contemporary societies between gender and consumption. Differences in gender consumption tendencies emerge during adolescence. One of the differences in adolescents regarding consumption because of gender is about physical appearance and clothes. Differences in tendencies may reflect physical and psychosocial maturity.

The socialization practices of families may also change depending on the gender of their adolescents. Gender characteristics also affect the use of mass media tools in adolescence. It has been observed that choices regarding the range of TV programmes, newspapers and periodicals are influenced by the gender factor. Girls display attitudes more in line with TV advertisements and have the ability to differentiate advertisements (Moschis and Churchill, 1979).

1.3.2.2 Socializing Factors

Environmental factors (family, school, friends, mass media tools and advertisements) play an important role in the socialization of the adolescent. These factors are also called *socializing agents.*

Family. This is the first and most effective instrument among socializing agents. The overall atmosphere in the family, family–adolescent relationships and the views of the adults about activities within the family are important factors for the adolescent to understand life and for development of their values (Martin and Turley, 2004).

The roles of adolescents within the family are determined. The adolescent adopts these roles either by observation or by the education provided by the family. Families provide their adolescents with direct opportunities to adopt their roles as customers by realizing their purchase demands, giving them pocket money and taking them shopping (John, 1999). Therefore, they teach their adolescents how to use money, buy quality goods and about price–quality relations, and thus have an influence on their adolescents' choices of brands (Ozgen, 1995; Shim and Gehrt, 1996).

The adolescent also observes the parents while they use credit cards or check expenditures by writing down on paper; thus the adolescent develops ideas as to how money is spent and put into bank accounts. Observing the use of coupons or similar tools during shopping by their families, the adolescent learns to be economic and sees the change of money resources in time (Martin and Oliva, 2001).

Families intentionally or unintentionally employ five different methods when teaching their adolescents how to be a customer. These are the following:

* prohibiting certain activities
* advising on consumption
* exchanging ideas on consumption decisions
* providing examples to the adolescent by their own behaviours, and
* allowing the adolescent to learn by his or her own experience.

(Dursun, 1993)

The degree and frequency of the family's communication with the adolescent affect indirectly the relationship he or she has with socializing agents in adopting customer information, skills and behaviours. The less the frequency of communication, the stronger the influence of TV advertisements and friends. Adolescents in such families gain their customer information from their friendship groups or mass media tools rather than their families. In families where adolescents can express their opinions more freely, they have more information on issues related to consumption. Adolescents of such families eliminate non-realistic elements in advertisements and have more information regarding diversity of products (McLeod, 1974).

CONCEPTUAL FRAMEWORK

Research on the topic of customer socialization is mainly based on two models: the "Cognitive Development Model" and the "Social Learning Model". The Cognitive Development Model explains that socialization is a function of changes in the cognitive structure that occur between infancy and adulthood. Piaget's Theory of Cognitive Development explains that as the adolescent grows older, he/she understands and responds to the world around him/her due to biological maturation and environmental experiences (Moschis and Churchill, 1978; Young, 2005). The social learning theory emphasizes socialization agents. It states that socialization takes place when the learner interacts with the socialization agents. The three elements of social learning theory are the Antecedent Variables, the Socialization Processes and the Outcomes (Moschis and Churchill, 1978).

1   Antecedent Variables
These are divided into two categories. The first category is "social structural variables". The social setting within which the interaction between the individual and socialization agent occurs is explained in terms of social structural variables like race, gender, social class and family size (Moschis and Churchill, 1978). These variables describe the demographic background of a person (Shim, 1996). In the present study the effect of socio-economic status and gender is investigated.

The second category is "age or life cycle position". The process of socialization is not limited to adolescence, but occurs throughout the life of every person (Belk, 1985). In the present study, adolescents among the age group of 10 to 16 years have been studied. Adolescence is a crucial and transitional period in the life of an individual. This is the period when changes occur in the behaviour and personality of an individual.

These antecedent variables influence learning of different customer skills. For example, it has been found that upper socio-economic class adolescents are able to manage finance better and are more likely to have economic orientations for consumption than adolescents belonging to a lower socio-economic class (Moschis and Churchill, 1978). Adolescents from upper socio-economic status are more oriented towards brands than adolescents from lower socio-economic classes (Moschis *et al.*, 1984b). One study reported that adolescents belonging to higher socio-economic class are more aware of the marketplace because they are more exposed to consumption opportunities as compared to the adolescents belonging to lower socio-economic status (Moschis and Moore, 1979). Likewise age and gender of an adolescent may also directly influence his/her customer skills. Older adolescents perform more socially desirable behaviour and are able to manage finance better than younger ones. Boys are more aware of customer matters, are more materialistic and have stronger social orientations for consumption than girls (Moschis and Churchill, 1978).

2   Socialization Processes
Socialization Processes includes both the "socialization agent" and "the type of learning" (Moschis and Churchill, 1978).

a   Socialization Agent
A socialization agent is "any person or organization directly involved in socialization because of frequency of contact with the learner, primacy over the individual, and control over rewards and punishments given to the person" (Belk, 1985). Socialization agents are "the sources of influence which transmit norms, attitudes, motivations, and behaviours to the learner; socialization is assumed to be taking place during the course of the person's interaction with these agents in various social settings" (Jorgensen and Savla, 2010).

Customer socialization agents play an important role in making adolescents learn the role of a customer. When an individual interacts with these agents, he/she learns the norms, skills, attitude and behaviour relevant to consumption from these agents. Social influence shapes the customer behaviour of adolescents by providing information and setting normative standards of conduct (Beyda, 2010). The socialization agents may not influence only during the purchase, but also before and after the purchase (Mangleburg *et al.*, 2004). The existent literature has revealed parents, peers, school and mass media as four main customer socialization agents. In the present study the influence of parents, peers, mass media (TV and internet) and school as customer socialization agents is investigated. These are discussed below:

1   **Parents as a customer socialization agent.** Parents are the most important socialization agent. Parents interact with their adolescents about consumption, take them on shopping trips. Thus, they help them

in learning the role of customer (Ward, 1972). Adolescents observe their parents when they use credit cards, use coupons while shopping. Hence, they learn how to spend money and to be economical (Martin and Oliva, 2001). By giving instructions to their adolescents, parents influence their financial knowledge (Drentea and Lavrakas, 2000; Lyons and Hunt, 2003; Cude *et al.*, 2006). Adolescents also learn about price–quality relations from their parents. Therefore, the parents help them to buy good quality products (Ozgen, 1995; Shim and Gehrt, 1996). According to Mizerski (1995) parents help their adolescents to learn the role of the customer in five different ways. These are: (1) prohibiting certain activities; (2) advising on consumption; (3) exchanging ideas on consumption decisions; (4) providing examples to the adolescent by their own behaviour; and (5) allowing the adolescent to learn by his or her own experience (Hayta, 2008).

Family as a socialization agent directly and indirectly influences the customer socialization of adolescents. Direct influence can be through various communication processes like social interaction, reinforcement and observation. Generally, limited attempts are made by the parents to teach customer skills to the adolescents. Parents expect that their adolescents should observe them and learn the customer role from them (Moschis, 1985). Effective customer behaviour may develop if positive reinforcement is given and development of effective customer behaviour may get restricted if negative reinforcement is given (Moschis *et al.*, 1984a). Most studies have focused on overt interaction about consumption, like Moschis *et al.* (1984a) and Ward and Wackman (1971).

Studies have also been conducted to see how structures and patterns of family communication influence the customer knowledge of adolescents. By influencing adolescents' interaction with other sources of customer influence, family indirectly influences their customer learning. For example, families with a socio-oriented communication structure encourage their adolescents to use mass media to learn how to behave in various social settings. Perhaps, due to this, adolescents develop a materialistic attitude as it is believed that adolescents learn the "expressive" aspects of consumption from mass media (Moore and Moschis, 1981). Parents also mediate the effects of other socialization agents especially TV (McLeod *et al.*, 1982).

The impact of TV advertising on customer learning has been found to be dependent on the frequency of interaction of the adolescent with his/her parents about consumption matters. The impact of TV advertising is stronger in families where discussions about consumption are less frequent (Moschis and Churchill, 1979; Moschis and Moore, 1982).

2 **Peers as a customer socialization agent.** Peers are defined as "belonging to the same societal group especially based on age, grade, or status" (www.merriam-webster.com/dictionary/peer). Peers are a very important source of influence for adolescents (Flouri, 2004). Every individual feels the need for social interaction with various people like their friends, classmates and members of formal organizations (Moschis, 1985). As the adolescent grows older, the importance of peers increases in his/her life. Peers fulfil their need for social acceptance. Peers help adolescents to make their own social identities. They influence the choice, preference and taste of adolescents. Adolescents become more aware about the different brands and products in the market by interacting more about consumption matters with their peers (Ozgen, 1995). Previous research suggests that adolescents learn the symbolic meaning associated with products from their friends. Adolescents use those products and brands which they feel will be approved by their peers. Adolescents learn from peers' "expressive elements of consumption" or "affective consumption" ("styles and moods of consumption") (Moschis and Churchill, 1978). Also, it has been found that peers play a vital role in the development of adolescents' preference for stores (McNeal, 1979), products (Hawkins and Coney, 1974), brands of selected products (Moschis *et al.*, 1984b) and things to collect (Baker and Gentry, 1996).

3 **Mass media as a customer socialization agent.** Mass media such as TV, radio, newspapers, internet etc. plays an important role in the customer socialization of adolescents. "No other agent of customer socialization has received more attention (in the literature) than mass media" (Moschis, 1985, p. 121). It has been recognized as a very prominent customer socialization agent in the marketing literature. For marketers, it is a very effective source of influencing people, as marketers believe that what is famous in the mass media becomes salient in the minds of the public and so influences their behaviour as customers (Sutherland and Galloway, 1981). Mass media is very effective in reaching customers and making them aware about products. It has been ranked as the most important source of new product information by Chinese adolescents (McNeal and Ji, 1999). TV advertising is an influential way of communicating messages to adolescents. Both advertising and editorial programming content of TV inform young people about products and influence their buying behaviour (Galst and White, 1976; O'Guinn and Shrum, 1997). TV advertising is the prime source of information for adolescents (Oates *et al.*, 2003).

In the whole world, internet use is increasing tremendously. The internet as a communication tool is a strong socialization agent (Lee *et al.*, 2003). The principal users are adolescents. The internet is the most used and powerful socialization agent (Singh *et al.*, 2003; Barber, 2013). It is an apt place for participating actively in the learning process and thus it promotes an "active" process of socialization (Lee and Conroy, 2005).

It is the main source of customer information and entertainment for adolescents (Rose *et al.*, 2009). People can find a variety of products easily on the internet with detailed information. Nowadays, adolescents spend long hours on the internet. The internet offers a new shopping experience. Lee *et al.* (2003) proposed that, "the internet has created a new learning culture, which is social in nature, allowing adolescents to share, discuss, influence and learn interactively from each other and from the medium" (p. 1709). The revolutionary internet era has come up with customer-generated media, like blogs, social networking sites etc., which can be used by marketers to reach customers (Ahmad *et al.*, 2011). Adolescents among the age group of 11–15 years are "early adopters" of new technologies (Ross and Harradine, 2004). As adolescents are the prime users of the internet, so their internet use is of great interest to researchers from different fields (Kaur and Medury, 2011). Advertisers are now adopting and making more use of the internet to connect with customers.

4   **School as a customer socialization agent.** School plays a major role in the socialization of adolescents. It is a place where an adolescent spends most of his/her productive time in a day. The role of teachers is as important as the role of family in developing customer behaviour of adolescents (Ozgen, 1995). Schooling directly affects adolescents' acquisition of knowledge and behaviour (Sylva, 1994). Stampfl *et al.* (1978) found that adolescents who received formal structured teaching have a better understanding of customer concepts than those who received open structured teaching. According to Flouri (2004), schools are responsible for "preparing the youth to function as adults by giving them the skill, attitude, and knowledge bases necessary for good citizenship and economic self-sufficiency". Nowadays, marketers are targeting schools to capture the young customer market. Companies sponsor the different activities in schools, organize workshops and seminars, distribute their pamphlets and free samples of their products, conduct educational programmes like awareness about health and nutrition, environmental issues, hygiene through sanitary items etc. Hence, schools in recent times serve not only academically but also provide commercial knowledge. When a company promotes its products in schools, this conveys a message to the students that the particular brand is trustworthy. Hence, schools influence the buying behaviour of adolescents.

b   Type of Learning

Another aspect of the socialization processes is the "type of learning". Moschis and Churchill (1978) described how individuals may learn from socialization agents through the process of modelling, reinforcement and social interaction. Modelling involves imitation of an agent's behaviour. Reinforcement can be positive or negative. Social interaction includes a combination of both modelling and reinforcement.

3   The Customer Skills or the Outcomes

Socialization agents help the young customer in learning customer behaviour and in acquiring the "Customer Skills" or the "Outcomes" (Ward and Wackman, 1971; Moore and Stephens, 1975). There are two types of customer skills as suggested by previous research: direct and indirect. "Direct" skills are directly relevant to purchasing and consumption. Examples of such skills include skills at budgeting and pricing, attitude towards market stimuli etc. The skills that are not directly relevant to purchase and consumption but motivate purchase or consumption are called "indirect" skills. Examples of such skills include materialism, social and economic orientations for consumption (Ward, 1974).

The skills examined in this study are customer affairs knowledge, customer activism, materialism, economic and social orientations for consumption and attitude towards market stimuli (including advertisements, brands, prices, stores and salespeople). The influence of various customer socialization variables on these customer skills is discussed below.

CUSTOMER AFFAIRS KNOWLEDGE AND CUSTOMER ACTIVISM

Several customers' groups have criticized marketers for their unethical practices and the effects of these on adolescents, considering them the most vulnerable segment of society. Young customers are a major market not only for snacks and sweets but also for expensive items (Halan, 2002). The Government of India, like responsible governments of other countries, aims to make customers aware of their rights and duties and to protect their interests. Despite many efforts to protect customers by the government, the customers and especially adolescents and adolescents as customers are being exploited by the marketers. The main reason for exploitation is the ignorance of customers. A customer who is aware of customer concepts and wisely uses the knowledge while performing customer behaviour is safe. Hence, the role of customer affairs knowledge and customer activism becomes important. Customer affairs knowledge includes basic knowledge about the quality, price, utility of products and knowledge about customer rights, duties and customer protection measures. Customer affairs knowledge has been defined as "cognitions held with respect to basic terms in economics, insurance, finance, real estate, and marketing; knowledge of customer legislation in the areas of unit pricing, bait advertising, code dating, and remedies available to customers" (Moschis and Churchill, 1978). Customer affairs knowledge plays an important role in the analysis of the products or services that customers want to buy (Cakarnis and D'Alessandro, 2015). Customer activism has been defined as "activities relating to socially desirable customer behaviour" (Moschis and Churchill, 1978). Various customer socialization variables influence customer affairs knowledge and customer activism.

Parents play a very important role in making adolescents aware of their basic customer rights (Mehta and Keng, 1985) and contributing to customer activism (Moschis *et al.*, 1984a). Peers have been found to be the most significant source of market knowledge (Mehta and Keng, 1985). TV commercials increase product and brand knowledge of adolescents (Moschis and Moore, 1978). Social utility reasons for watching TV shows (like "to learn what things to buy to make good impression on others" and "to find out what kind of products to buy to become/feel like those people I wish I were") are found to be related positively to customer affairs knowledge (Moschis and Churchill, 1978). Schooling directly affects adolescents' acquisition of knowledge and behaviour (Sylva, 1994).

Adolescents who receive formal structure teaching have a better understanding of customer concepts than those who receive open structure teaching (Stampfl *et al.*, 1978). Adolescents belonging to upper socioeconomic class have more opportunities for consumption; hence they may be more aware of customer concepts (Ward, 1974). These adolescents are more likely to obtain information before making customer decisions and therefore shop smartly (Moschis and Churchill, 1978). The results of various previous studies like Moschis (1976), Moschis and Churchill (1978, 1979), Moschis and Moore (1978) and Moschis *et al.*, (1984a) revealed that boys have more customer affairs knowledge compared to girls and perform customer activism more frequently. In a study it has been found that boys are more concerned about the environment and are ready to pay extra for environment friendly products (Yadav and Pathak, 2014).

MATERIALISM

Materialistic individuals tend to concentrate only on material possessions. Materialism has been defined differently by authors. Belk (1985) defined three traits of materialism as possessiveness, no generosity and envy. Another definition is given by Richins and Dawson (1992), "as a personal value" such that people who are more materialistic have "acquisition at the center of their lives", "view these [possessions] as essential to their satisfaction and well-being in their life" and "tend to judge their own and other's success by the number and quality of possessions accumulated".

Different socialization agents are responsible for inculcating materialism among adolescents. Adolescents who belong to those families where the interaction between parents and adolescents is less frequent, are often more oriented towards material things (Moschis and Moore, 1978). Social utility reasons for watching TV shows (like "to learn what things to buy to make a good impression on others" and "to find out what kind of products to buy to become/feel like those people I wish I were") have been found to be positively related to materialism (Moschis and Churchill, 1978). Previous research suggests that adolescents learn "expressive" elements of consumption from their peers and TV (Reisman and Roseborough, 1955). This speculation is supported by many studies (Moschis and Churchill, 1978; Churchill and Moschis, 1979). Materialistic values increase with the amount of TV viewing and peer communication (Churchill and Moschis, 1979). Previous research studies have also found the relationship between materialism and demographic and socio-economic variables. For example, boys have been found to be more materialistic as compared to girls in many studies (Moschis and Churchill, 1978; Churchill and Moschis, 1979).

ECONOMIC AND SOCIAL ORIENTATIONS FOR CONSUMPTION

Orientation or motivation within an individual is the driving force that urges them to act. The first type of orientation studied is the "economic orientations for consumption", which is defined as "cognitive orientation related to the importance of product functional and economic features; orientations toward comparison shopping and significant discriminatory attributes' (Moschis and Churchill, 1978).

Another type is the "social orientations for consumption". It has been defined as "cognitive orientations related to the importance of conspicuous consumption; and self-expression via conspicuous consumption" (Moschis and Churchill, 1978). Conspicuous consumption is "the tendency for individuals to enhance their image, through overt consumption of possessions, which communicates status to others" (O'Cass and McEwen, 2004, p. 34). In many developing countries, owning and conspicuous show-off of luxuries is a key part of contemporary lifestyles (Bian and Forsythe, 2012). Nowadays, stature and prestige concerns are shaping buying behaviour (O'Cass and McEwen, 2004; Goldsmith *et al.*, 2010). Adolescents are aware of the ideas of conspicuous products/services, as a means of self-expression (Phau and Cheong, 2009; O'Cass and Siahtiri, 2013).

Researchers have found a significant relationship between various socialization variables and orientations for consumption. Parents have been found to influence economic orientations (Moschis and Churchill, 1978; Churchill and Moschis, 1979) and social orientations (Moschis and Moore, 1979). In one study it was reported that adolescents who feel less parental care and those who spend more time using media are more likely to consume conspicuously (Gudmunson and Beutler, 2012). Adolescents learn "expressive elements of consumption" (like social orientations for consumption) from peers (Moschis and Churchill, 1978; Churchill and Moschis, 1979). Peers have a major influence on a young customer's buying decision making of luxury products (Lachance *et al.*, 2003). TV enhances social orientations. Adolescents learn "expressive elements of consumption" from TV (Moschis and Churchill, 1978; Churchill and Moschis, 1979).

Social and economic orientations for consumption also vary with respect to demographic variables. As an adolescent grows, social development takes place and adolescents start making social comparisons. Their ability to understand the social meaning of products increases (John, 1999). Gudmunson and Beutler (2012) found age to be significantly related to conspicuous consumption. Also, economic orientations for consumption increase with age (Moschis and Moore, 1978; Churchill and Moschis, 1979; Moschis and Churchill, 1979; Moore and Moschis, 1981). Upper socio-economic class adolescents have more economic orientations for consumption (Moschis and Churchill, 1978). Boys have more social orientation for consumption than girls (Churchill and Moschis, 1979; O'Cass

Table 1.2 Family Communication Patterns

		Concept-Oriented Communication	
		Low	High
Socio-Oriented Communication	**Low**	**Laissez-faire** Little/no parent–adolescent communication	**Pluralistic** Open communication and discussion of idea without insisting on obedience to authority
	High	**Protective** Stress obedience and social harmony	**Consensual** Encourages adolescent interest in outside world as long as it doesn't disturb the internal harmony of the family

Source: Moschis, 1985.

and McEwen, 2004). Contradicting this, a study by Stokburger-Sauer and Teichmann (2013) concluded that girls have a more positive attitude towards luxury brands than boys.

Peer group. Peer groups are important socializing factors that contribute to effective learning about consumption elements such as monetary values and social motivation. An adolescent's friends influence his or her consumption by making him or her familiar with products and brands, changing his or her beliefs and information on the product, helping him or her to try products, teaching him or her how to use the product, and showing how his or her needs can be met with what product (Ozgen, 1995).

The wish to belong to a group or to be accepted by the group may require the adolescent to learn or perform different actions or behaviours. When certain products and brands that are significant for adolescents become prominent in adolescent groups, positive feelings and materialist values develop in each of the group members for these products and brands. There are studies that suggest that adolescents learn the symbolic meaning of most of the products from their friends (Opree *et al.*, 2014).

School. School is a very important socialization factor in the adolescence period. Adolescents spend more time in school than they do with their parents both in the pre-college period and later in their school lives. The adolescent spends more time at school with the teacher and friends than he or she does with the family. School, which is a social institution, is expected to reflect the requirements and objectives of society and to provide young individuals with necessary knowledge and skills about consumption. In this period, teachers play as important role as families in shaping the adolescents' consumption behaviours (Ozgen, 1995). Introductory information provided at school regarding economic culture has important effects on the adolescent in terms of gaining information, skills and behaviours related to consumption (Nusair *et al.*, 2010).

Advertisements and mass media tools. Although families play a primary role in socialization of adolescents as customers, no other socializing agent attracts more attention than mass media in adolescents' customer behaviour literature. Mass media such as TV, radio, newspapers, periodicals and the internet are media that play important roles in the socialization of the adolescents as customers. Adolescents learn many basic issues related to consumption from messages addressed to them by marketing experts through mass media advertising. It is well known that TV advertisements help adolescents to gain information on brands, store, and products and affect their consumption behaviours. TV advertising is more effective on adolescents because of its combination of sound and image. In France, including the advertisements before and after the news, an adolescent of 8 to 14 years watches 10 to 20 advertisements daily, thus 3600 to 7000 advertisements a year (Chia, 2010).

The basic role of TV advertisements is to provide customers with sufficient and true information about products and services, reach people who cannot be reached by the salesperson and educate the customer. It is designed to influence customer behaviour either by encouraging customers principally to switch from one brand to another or to remain loyal to the one they currently buy. To some extent, advertising may also be concerned with creating markets for new brands. Advertising experts operate to reach adolescents by directly addressing adolescents who have their own money or encouraging adolescents to approach their parents with requests to purchase items. However, the influence of advertisement decreases in the cases where families spend more time with their adolescents and intervene in these messages (McNeal, 1979).

Indeed, advertisements have different effects on adolescents of different ages, because there is a direct relationship between the age and general comprehension capabilities of adolescents. Therefore, the increase in general comprehension capabilities in parallel with growth in age helps adolescents to identify advertisements from various perspectives and to develop various defence mechanisms. For this reason, it is natural that an advertisement that influences adolescents of 8 years does not influence those of 12 years. However, an important aspect that should not be ignored is that adolescents of the same age can perceive the same advertisement differently (Sun and Wu, 2004).

A study on this issue asked 250 adolescents of different age groups what they wanted for Christmas: 67% of those in the 7 to 8 age group, 49% of those of the 9 to 10 age group and 40% of those in the 11 to 12 age group said that they wanted a product that had been advertised on TV at least once (Valkenburg and Buijzen, 2005).

As many advertisements broadcast on TV are the creation of brilliant minds, which aim to persuade people for purchase the product advertised, most of the messages advertised get into the minds of customers due to the beautiful audio and visual effects. They direct the attention of adolescents to more striking and dashing products by promoting the items in a way that leads the adolescent to think that possession of the product will attract others' attention and they will be taken seriously by others. Advertising is criticized on the basis that sometimes it encourages customers to buy things that they do not need or sometimes to wastefulness. Thus, it may be argued that advertisements develop in adolescents the desire for whatever product they see, and this creates the spendthrift and wasteful type of customer (Brucks *et al.*, 2002).

1.3.2.3 Learning Mechanisms

Research on factors involved in socializing the customer focuses on cognitive development and social learning theories.

Cognitive development theory. The cognitive development of adolescents is about the process of organization of their skills and the information they obtained as to how to use what they had learned from their surroundings and how to develop interpersonal relations. This will help them not only to see their world from a multiple perspective but also to play their roles as customers. The most important theory related to cognitive development that is acceptable is that of Swiss psychologist Jean Piaget.

Social learning processes. Social learning theory argues for the importance of learning by observation in human life. During the socializing process, members of society are educated in socially accepted behaviours and gender roles. The individual creates standards for self-evaluation, although at the same time, he or she takes standards from the observed models as examples. This theory transcends traditional behaviourism and argues that all individual and environmental factors have effects as cross-cutting determinants. It covers observation learning reinforcing and social interaction.

Observational learning. Adolescents constantly observe the behaviours of others (socializing agents) and the outcomes of these behaviours. Although they imitate the reinforced behaviours that they observe, they do not imitate those that do not have a positive outcome for them. Thus, adolescents learn by observing the family's attitudes and behaviours related to consumption and their ways of receiving money. Adolescents pay attention to their parents' discussions about consumption and patterns of shopping and spending money, who pays the bills and who keeps the records and, thus, learn patterns of saving and spending (Nazık and Nakılcıoğlu, 2002).

Reinforcing. The learning process by reinforcing is based on the mechanisms of reward or punishment. The individual will repeat the behaviours for which he or she was rewarded in the past by socializing agents and will refrain from repeating those for which he or she received punishment. Support given by the family for behaviour of the adolescent provides a positive reinforcement for him or her, whereas punishment for a behaviour that they do not find appropriate, such as being prohibited from watching TV or seeing friends, will provide a negative reinforcement. Buying a product desired by the adolescent as a reward for positive behaviour or denying the adolescent the product or gift he or she desires for bad behaviour significantly shapes the adolescent's behaviour and also influences the adolescent's attitudes to these products.

Social interaction. This affects the norms, attitudes and behaviours of the adolescent related to his or her relationships with other individuals in society. Both observational and reinforcement behaviours can be observed in social interaction. Communication patterns between the parents and their adolescent can be given as examples of learning by social interaction. Parents can give consumption information to the adolescent during a discussion on consumption. The family talking to the adolescent about the expensiveness of a product as compared to another product will help the adolescent to get an idea about prices. The adolescent will also gain much information on consumption concepts such as product–quality relations and brands by social interaction with his or her friends or family.

1.4 Model of Family Decision Making

Family decision making is different from individual decision making, since it involves more individuals and is more complex because of the chance of joint decisions between family members and the different role specifications for the members in the process of decisions (Assael, 1992).

Joint decision making is more likely to occur in the following situations (Sheth, 1974):

1   When the level of perceived risk in buying is high. A wrong decision could affect the whole family; therefore the joint decision is made to prevent risk and uncertainty. Buying a house is a good example in this case, since it involves financial risks, social risks in terms of interaction with neighbours, as well as psychological risks.
2   When the purchasing decision is more important to the family. This second point is closely related to the first one, "importance is associated with risk". In a decision to buy a car, either to buy a family car or an individual car: which importance comes first?
3   When there are few or no time pressures. More time available creates more possibilities for joint decision making. On the other hand when there is time pressure, one of the family members will forced to make the purchase decision. Time pressures are less when there is only one employed parent in the family.

There are five roles that could be played by members of the family, and each member may take more than one role or no role at all. Five roles are shown in Table 1.3 (Sheth, 1974).

1   The information gatherer (gatekeeper), influences the family's processing of information by controlling the level and type of stimuli

Table 1.3 Role of Family Members in Different Product Categories

	Personal Products	Family Toiletries	Household Durables	Family Automobiles	Consumables	Financial Products	Vacations	Educational Products
Father	Passive users	Decider/ buyer	Passive users / User/ initiator/ gatekeeper	Decider/ buyer / User	Decider/ buyer / Co-decider/ initiator/ influencers	Passive users / Influencers	Decider/ buyer / Co-decider/ buyer/ gatekeeper	Initiator / Influencer / Decider/ buyer / Influencer/ buyers
Mother	Buyer	Decider/ influencer	User / Influencer/ decider	User / Influencers/ co-decider	Passive users / Influencers/ co-decider	Decider/ buyer / Initiator	Passive users / Influencers/ co-decider	Decider/ buyer / Co-deciders / Influencer / Co-deciders
Adolescents	Users / Influencers/ co-decider	Users / Influencers/ co-decider	Users / Buyers	Influencers / Initiator/ gatekeeper	Users / Co-deciders/ users	Users / Influencer	Influencer / Co-deciders/ users	Influencers / Co-deciders / Initiator / Co-deciders

Source: *Business Today*, 8(4), 22 February to 6 March 1999.

the family is exposed to. The information gatherer has the most expertise in obtaining and evaluating information from diverse sources and is mainly aware of alternative sources of information.

2   The influencer establishes the decision criteria by which products are compared (price, quality, etc.) and influences other family members' evaluation of products. The influencer might or might not be the same person as the information gatherer.

3   The decision maker decides which brand or product to purchase, since this person has the power to approve the final decision.

4   The purchasing agent carries out the decision by purchasing the product for the family. The purchasing agent might or might not be the same person as the decision maker. The decision maker might delegate the purchasing agent to buy the products for the family.

5   The (end) customer, who uses the product and evaluates it, giving some feedback to other family members regarding the satisfaction with the chosen brand and desirability to purchase the same brand or product again. In this study, adolescents will be observed and analysed as the influencer without neglecting other roles that might be played by adolescents during the family decision making process. Adolescents might act as the decision maker where both parents have no time to manage the household and therefore delegate all the decision to adolescents themselves.

1.5 Understanding Adolescents' Influence

The theory about adolescents' influence is very important because it helps explain the role of adolescents in family decision making. One important theory that explores adolescents' role in the family is "Resources Theory". Resources are the main source of power. A resource is defined as anything that one partner may make available to another, helping the latter satisfy his or her needs or attain his or her goals.

McDonald (1980) proposes five types of resources that serve as bases from which family members may derive power. They are normative, economic, affective, personal and cognitive resources. Normative resources include a family's values and norms. Economic resources refer to the monetary control exerted by the income earner. Affective resources cover interpersonal relationships and belongingness. Personal resources encompass physical appearance and role competence. Cognitive resources include the intelligence of family members. Parents might exercise the normative and economic resources, whereas the adolescent is using the affective and cognitive resources in family decision making.

Resource theory provides a basis in family decision making and group decision making research. Power, which is closely connected with the resource, is defined as a capacity or an ability to influence others. Power is linked to the family and an individual's specific role in the family. The definition of "influence" varies from one person to another. Some people perceive influence only as the active dimension and others perceive it as both passive and active. Cartwright (1999) defines influence as "a conjecture when one person acts in such a way as to change the behaviour of another in some intended manner". Active influence is also called direct influence, where adolescents exert direct influence over parental spending when they request specific products and brands. Direct influence also refers to joint decision making, actively participating with family members to make a purchase or suggesting that other family members select or choose a product or certain brands of products.

Adolescents' influence may also be passive, where there is no evidence of speech or overt actions on the part of an adolescent. Passive influence is also called indirect influence, where parents are aware of what the adolescent wants and try to comply without direct interaction with the adolescent, and it occurs when parents buy products and brands that they know their adolescents prefer, without being asked or told to make that specific purchase (Hawkins, 1977). The prior knowledge that the parents have about the taste and preferences of adolescents creates the passive buying patterns of the adolescents. According to Cartwright, an influencer in a family does not necessarily have expertise, and he/she can influence one or more of the decision making stages in varying roles and with varying impacts. Influences are distributed in two types: (1) based on decision stages (idea generation, choice of alternatives, etc.); and (2) based on decision areas (type, brand, price and shop).

Certain products are simply adolescents' products for which they are the primary users or buyers, such as cereal. Other products used by other family members could be influenced by adolescents. Adolescents are trained to be the future loyal customer. A lot of companies, especially food companies, have a long-term strategy of enlightening adolescents' loyalties, by introducing their company's brand and product awareness from the early age of the adolescent, with the expectation that adolescents will be familiar with their products by the time they get older. It is the goal of the advertisers to make adolescents not only aware of the product, but also to make the brand stay and grow with them.

1.6 Why Do Marketers Target Adolescents?

Retailers and manufacturers have two sources of new customers: those whom they can persuade to change from their competitors and those who have not yet entered the market. Those who switch are less likely to be loyal than those who are nurtured from adolescence. Marketers pay special attention to adolescents, and the latter are considered by the former as the most vulnerable audiences of society because they enjoy advertisements to the maximum. Industry spending on advertising to adolescents has exploded in the past decade, increasing from a mere $100 million in 1990 to more than $2.5 billion in 2005. The repetition of TV advertisements leaves a mark on young minds. Previous research showed that adolescents are more likely to make requests for products which are frequently consumed by them, such as breakfast cereals, snacks or sweets, or for products that are of particular interest to them, such as toys or those with special offers. Marketers targeted them as future customers, by making them comfortable with a brand name. That an adolescent makes his or her first brand and category choice in a school canteen, when he or she is hardly 4 or 5, makes it clear the impact TV advertisement on brand recognition of adolescents (Valkenburg and Buijzen, 2005).

Adolescents initially take advertisements as entertainment and, being innocent and gullible, force their parents to purchase a product. This called a "Nag Factor". Parents today are willing to buy much more for their young children due to certain factors, such as smaller family size, dual incomes and postponing giving adolescents choices until later in life. All this means that families have more disposable income. Also, guilt plays a role in spending decisions as time-stressed parents try to substitute material goods for less time spent with their young children. Moreover, due to the fact that adolescents' personal spending is also on the rise, marketers are showing great interests in this segment. Research states that adolescents under 12 years of age spend an estimated $25 billion and, through their parents, may influence another $200 billion of spending per year (Strasburger, 2001). Adolescents spend an estimated $140 billion a year on food and beverages and one of the latest estimates on spending by adolescents in the United States suggests that adolescents of 12 years and under spend $27.9 billion of their own income, while they influence approximately $249 billion of their parents' finances (Lawlor and Prothero, 2003) provides a solid ground for marketers to target adolescents. They are discovering that there's lots of money to be made by treating adolescents like teenagers. The marketing industry is forcing adolescents to grow up quickly.

It is not just in the United States that adolescents that are targets of advertisers, but adolescents in virtually every country of the world (Chan, 2013). Rose (1999) estimates that there are over 200 million adolescents from 5 to 14 years of age in the countries of Japan, South Korea and the People's Republic of China. The Population Reference Bureau estimates the population of adolescents worldwide to be 32% of the total world population. McNeal and Ji (1999) note, "there are nearly 2 billion adolescents below the age of 15 worldwide, making the adolescents of the world a handsome market for advertisers". Of course, adolescents may not give full attention to the screen during advertisement breaks, but, unlike most of the adults, they do not mentally switch off when advertisements appear on TV. Taking into consideration these numbers, there is little wonder why adolescents have become a target market, and why advertisers spend large amounts of funds on advertising to adolescents.

1.7 Adolescents' Influence Efforts

In an attempt to get their parents to meet their purchase request and play a significant role in the family's purchase decision making, adolescents make use of a number of influence efforts. From a customer socialization perspective it is highly significant to know how adolescents learn ways to become successful influence agents through the use of increasingly sophisticated influence efforts. With increase in age, they become more verbal in their request and ask for the products by name, sometimes requesting, demanding, begging or screaming to get what they want. It is also important for marketers to identify the most effective and the least effective influence efforts. The most effective influence efforts will be those reported as being the most successful in getting the adolescent what he/she wants, while the least effective will be those reported as not working at all in getting him/her what he/she wants. Comprehensive influence efforts are used by adolescents to affect the outcome of a family's purchase decision. In response to adolescents' purchase requests, parents do not always agree to getting them the things asked for. They also respond in various ways. Further, efforts have been made to identify the parents' responses to adolescents' purchase requests.

The present study would try to reveal the relationship between the adolescents' influence efforts and the parents' response.

1.8 Conflicts in the Family Decision Making Process

Whenever there are two or more people involved in decision making, some conflicts might occur. Refusal to comply with the preference from other family members would mostly lead to conflicts. Even though serious conflict in the family decision making process is considered infrequent, some types of family conflict are highly possible because of the differences in the preferences and choices from each family member (Sheth, 1974). Sheth stated that the conflict between family members is because of the existence of different cognitive structures, which may include different purchase motives (reasons for buying a product) and evaluative beliefs (perceptions about alternatives). When several alternatives are being considered, each family member would endeavour to influence the other towards his or her preferred decision. Moreover, the differences in the interest of a purchase outcome would probably lead to disagreement or conflict.

In Belch *et al.*'s (1985) study, they found that the amount of disagreement is relatively low for decisions such as where to buy and when to buy, but it is higher when it comes to how much money to spend. Conflict can be managed in two ways: by either using avoidance tactics or resolution tactics. Since adolescents influence more on the product types, the nature of the product can also be significant in determining the choice of conflict resolution strategy, such as through bargaining. Bargaining involves some give and take. On the other hand, conflict avoidance was most commonly utilized for family products. Davis (1976) states that families quite often bargain, compromise and coerce rather than problem-solve in arriving at decisions. Davis used two models of decision strategies in dealing with conflicts: persuasion and bargaining. Persuasion is an act of demanding others do something by using emotional techniques such as crying in order for others to follow what he or she wants. When family members have different buying motives, they might approach the bargaining strategy. Bargaining influence tactics comprise waiting for the next purchase, impulse purchasing and procrastination. Family members recognize that there is a conflict between them and they try to solve it in fairness and equity.

1.9 Adolescents' Influence in the Parents' Decision Making Process

Family decision making research was initially directed by spouses, but "recent changes in demographic and household structure have increased adolescents' impact both on parents' purchasing decisions and the family decision making process" (Ekstrom *et al.*, 1987). Adolescents today, are seen as different from the past generation; especially 8–14 year olds. They have grown up faster, are better connected, more direct and well informed. They have more personal power, more money, more influence and more attention from parents than any other generation before them (Wu, 2003). The amount adolescents spend in family purchase decisions has risen over the last 40 years (Segal and Podoshen, 2013). The data monitor reports that adolescents were no longer satisfied with snacks and sweets, instead they were longing for entertainment along with food.

Adolescents' influence differs by the stage of decision making process (i.e. problem recognition, information seekers and choice) and product category. For a few products, they are information seekers, active initiators and buyers, whereas for other categories of product, they influence the parents' purchases (Kaur and Medury, 2011). Today's adolescents have more autonomy and power in decision making within the family and are vocal about what they want their parents to buy. From buying white goods and cars to cell phones and groceries, and even insurance policies, adolescents under the age of 13 are deciding which brands their parents should or should not buy.

There are several other reasons why adolescents are becoming so important in parents' buying decision making. First, nowadays parents are having fewer adolescents, and, for this reason, they tend to give each adolescent more possessions and more allowances in buying things. Second, there is an increasing number of one-parent households in which the adolescent is expected to be more involved in the household decision making. Third, having adolescents is often postponed until later in life when parents' careers are well established. With this condition, adolescents could participate more in planning purchases.

Finally, in most of the households where both of the parents are working, adolescents are empowered to contribute more to buying decision making. Determining what is needed in the household becomes the adolescents' responsibility. Therefore, the real customer for marketers nowadays is almost never the parent anymore. Adolescents are the buyer,

Table 1.4 Trends in the Customer Market

No.	Details
1	Changing demographic environment, where the 75 million "baby boomers" (born after the Second World War) now account for about one-third of the total population.
2	People marry later in life and have fewer adolescents.
3	The number of married couples continues to decline.
4	The number of working women is increasing dramatically.
5	About 65% of women will be in the labour force by 2005.
6	47% of all households will be non-family or single parent households by the year 2005.
7	Younger adults move out of their parents' home earlier in life.
8	The divorce rate is increasing.
9	The percentage of the more educated people is increasing.
10	People are becoming increasingly health conscious.
11	People generally live longer.

Source: Marketing and Sales Management, Business Management Club, 2001.

spender and decision maker, not only for adolescents' products but also for the household and their parents' other necessities. Adolescents tend to have more "say" in the products that are less expensive and for their own use because of changing trends in the economy.

In light of such high importance of adolescents' role in family buying decision making, it becomes important for marketers to appeal to the adult purchaser, as well as to the young children who influence them. Young children don't think like adults and they don't buy like adults. But they certainly have pull. Adolescents can dominate family life. They can influence – even veto – their parents' purchases of everything from cars to toys to groceries as well as determine their houschold's TV and entertainment choices. Adolescents' impact on familial spending adds up to billions of dollars every year.

In the present study an attempt has been made to examine the influence of adolescents in family buying decision making, with regard to variety of products ranging from adolescents' major products, adolescents' minor products, family major products, to family minor products.

1.10 Tools Used to Target Adolescents

a Building Brand Name Loyalty

In her book *No Logo*, Naomi Klein says that the mid-1980s saw the birth of a new kind of corporation – Nike, Calvin Klein, Tommy Hilfiger, to name a few – which changed their primary corporate focus from producing products to creating an image for their brand name. Marketers plant the seeds of brand recognition in very young adolescents, with the hope that the seeds will grow into lifetime relationships. According to the centre for a New American Dream, babies as young as 6 months of age can form mental images of corporate logos and mascots. Brand loyalties can be established as early as age 2, and by the time adolescents head off to school, most can recognize hundreds of brand logos.

b Buzz or Street Marketing

Many companies are using "buzz marketing" a new twist on the tried-and-tested "word of mouth" method. The idea is to find the coolest young children in a community and have them use or wear your product in order to create a buzz around it. Buzz, or "Street Marketing", can help a company to successfully connect with the savvy and elusive teen market by using trendsetters to give their products "cool" status.

c Commercialization in Education

A school used to be a place where adolescents were protected from the advertising and customer messages that permeated their world, but not anymore. Corporations realize the power of the school environment for promoting their names and products. A school setting delivers a captive youth audience and implies the endorsement of teachers and the educational system. Marketers are eagerly exploiting this medium in a number of ways, including:

- supplying schools with technology in exchange for high company visibility;
- exclusive deals with fast food or soft drink companies to offer their products in a school;
- advertising posted in classrooms, school buses, on computers etc. in exchange for funds;
- sponsoring school events.

d The Internet
The internet is an extremely desirable medium for marketers to target adolescents:

- It is part of youth culture. This generation of young people is growing up with the internet as a daily and routine part of their lives.
- Parents generally do not understand the extent to which adolescents are being marketed to online.
- Young children are often online alone, without parental supervision.
- Sophisticated technologies make it easy to collect information from young people for marketing research and to target individual adolescents with personalized advertising.
- By creating engaging, interactive environments based on product and brand names companies can build brand loyalties at an early age.
- Young children represent important demographics to marketers because they have their own purchasing power, exercise greater influence over family buying decision making and they are the adult customers of the future.

1.10.1 Three Markets in One

Adolescents constitute the most lucrative market for many businesses because they represent three markets in one.

- Adolescents are a current market because they have their own money to spend. They are viewed as having needs, having money to spend on items that satisfy their needs and having a willingness to spend money. Not only do producers of soft drinks, toys, cereals etc. treat them as a current market but outlets such as video game parlours and movie houses also treat adolescents as a ready market.

- Adolescents also constitute a market of influencers that cause billions of dollars of purchases among their parents. Marketers advertise the product to adolescents on TV, which directly or indirectly encourages them to persuade their parents to buy those products.
- Adolescents are a future market for most goods and services. Manufacturers and retailers respond to them as future customers to be cultivated now. Manufacturers of branded products (Nike, Adidas, Reebok etc.) try to attract adolescents because they know that today's adolescent is a customer of tomorrow.

1.10.2 Customer Socialization of Adolescents

Customer socialization is the process by which adolescents acquire skills, knowledge and attitudes relevant to their functioning in the marketplace. Adolescents learn about purchasing and consumption primarily from their parents. While TV may have a persuasive influence on what adolescents see and how they react to certain brands, the family is an instrument in teaching young people rational aspects of consumption, including basic customer needs. The parents always try to teach their adolescents to be more effective customers.

- Parents teach price–quality relations to their adolescents, including experience with the use of money and ways to shop for quality products.
- Parents teach their adolescents how to be effective comparison shoppers and how to buy products on sale.
- Parents influence adolescents' brand preferences.
- Parents have influenced adolescents' ability to distinguish fact from exaggeration in advertising.

Adolescents watch and imitate parental behaviour because parents serve as role models. Parents also co-shop with adolescents because they seek to expose adolescents to the experiences associated with visiting stores and use these occasions to teach adolescents customer skills. Adolescents are also socialized through direct experience. The increase in dual earning and single parent households has resulted in adolescents often shopping on their own. As a result, the process of customer socialization is occurring much earlier and much faster than it used to. TV and increasing commercialization of education in schools are also important sources of socialization: the greater the adolescents' exposure to TV, the greater the likelihood that they will accept the images and associations seen. In addition to this, younger adolescents may emulate older adolescents' behaviour and, in doing so, develop consumption skills. The adolescents' peer group can also affect customer socialization by influencing brand preferences and purchases.

So, on the whole, the role of adolescents in the household structure is undergoing a change. Today, adolescents are very fast and bright and they keep themselves abreast of changes in their environment. They are still the centre of the universe in the Indian family system and can actually pull the parents to visit a place time and again. Adolescents are an enormously powerful medium for relationship building in India. They not only influence markets in terms of parental decision making to buy certain kind of products, they are also future customers.

1.11 Significance of the Study

Adolescents, today, have huge influence on their parents' purchases. Parents, today, have a larger income and a higher education level; there are more single parent families, more liberalization in the parent–adolescent relationship, which has resulted into more open negotiation between parent and adolescent rather than a relationship regulated by authority and command. As a consequence, adolescents nowadays are receiving more love and attention from both parents and have been described as "Little Emperors and Empresses" (Cheng, 1993). The importance of family research has been recognized since Sheth (1974) highlighted the role of family rather than the individual as the basic unit of consumption. Traditionally, studies in family customer decision making focused on the husband–wife interaction (Segal and Podoshen, 2013). More recent studies have acknowledged that adolescents have an important role to play in the consumption activities of the family. Shoham and Dalakas (2005) reported that adolescents under 12 years old influence some $320 billion dollars' worth of household products. According to available industry data, the chocolate and confectionary market is estimated at 1300 crore/$290 million, the apparel market at 480 crore/$110 million and young children's footwear at 1000 crore/$220 million. In addition to this, 54% of India is estimated to be under the age of 25. So, adolescents are extremely important for marketers and customer researchers as they influence present and future consumption trends in number of ways.

> Young children do have needs that must be satisfied. In fact, as far as we know these are the some needs as those of adults. Given the

chance, the adolescents will select products and services that best satisfy their needs.

(McNeal, 1992, p. 350)

The following facts are given by James U. McNeal (1999) in his book *The Kids Market: Myths and Realities* emphasized the role of adolescents in family buying decision making.

1 "More Earners per Young Children": as women entered the workforce in great numbers in the 1970s, putting money in the household that was not there before.
2 "Fewer Young Children per Family": as the fertility rate decreases each year and women elect to have fewer adolescents (more money is allotted per adolescent).
3 "More Older and Wealthier Parents": as delaying having adolescents by career-minded couples seems to give adolescents much more importance when they do arrive.
4 "Fractured Families": an increase in fractured/splintered families as one in six adolescents is someone's step adolescent (they get more from more individuals).
5 "Single-Parent Households": adolescents in single-parent households often make their first purchase. More single-parent households where young children must participate in household activities (handling money and shopping).
6 "Grandparents Became More Important": as parents become busier and away from their adolescents more, grandparents started stepping in to help out. So, grandparents have become more important as, when both parents work or the single parent works, grandparents "fill in the gap" (this generation of grandparents is wealthier than the last).
7 "More Guilt on Part of Parents": more guilt on the part of the working dual-earner couples or the single-parent earner, thus quality time has been replaced by buying the adolescent something.
8 "Greater Concern": for the adolescents' future; as political, economic and global uncertainty abound, parents are giving more to their adolescents.

Besides acting as buyers with their own money to spend, adolescents directly or indirectly influence the purchase of a large variety of products. Marketing practitioners are increasing their efforts to grasp this market, whereas customer researchers are striving to identify the mechanisms underlying the influence of adolescents on household buying decision making. Understanding adolescents' influence in the family buying process has been acknowledged as an area in immense need of research. Marketers promote products with adult appeal to young children who are growing up earlier. Also, marketers have become increasingly interested in adolescents as customers; this has an impact on the ever-increasing volume of advertisements targeted at adolescents. Families' communication pattern has become more open and democratic. Parents pay more attention to their adolescents.

Adolescents have become "Dream adolescents" and "Trophy adolescents", holding a special status in the family. New behavioural patterns are arising, such as adolescents being influencers and participators in family decision making; and new media (e.g. digital and interactive) enters the market, and adolescents adopt this fast. Indian society vastly differs from the West in terms of family composition, family type and structure, norms, values and behaviour. It is important to understand adolescents' influence in purchase decision making in families in the Indian context. The buying power of adolescents in India is different compared to Western countries but still they play a key role in Indian families. The studied literature also showed a gap in studies related to young adolescents. Adolescents and tweens are not only important as individual customers but also as an influencing market directing parents' spending towards their own wants and needs – or as the advertising industry says, adolescents have "pester power". It would be interesting to see the results of a study with such young adolescents. Therefore, keeping in view the significance of the subject, there is a need to examine the impact of adolescents on family buying decision making. Hence, the present study, *Adolescents, Family and Consumer Behaviour: A Behavioural Study of Adolescents in Indian Urban Families*, has been planned to study the role and influence of adolescents in Indian urban families while purchasing.

1.12 Chapter Scheme

Chapter 1: Introduction
In this chapter, the significance of adolescents and their role in buying decision making in the family set-up is discussed.

Chapter 2: Adolescents' Role in Buying Decision Making
The detailed literature on adolescents' role in buying decision making is elaborated.

Chapter 3: Research Methodology
The design of the study emphasizes the methodology adopted for analysing and synthesizing the collected information through questionnaires.

Chapter 4: Data Analysis and Interpretation
The information obtained through questionnaires is analysed for studying adolescents' role in buying decision making. The results of the questionnaires are synthesized to analyse adolescents' influence in decision making and parents' perception towards their role in buying decision making.

Chapter 5: Conclusions and Future Scope of Work
The conclusions derived from the synthesis of the data in a sequential manner are presented, limitations of the study are highlighted and the scope for future work is also suggested.

2   Adolescents' Role in Buying Decision Making

No research can be conducted in a vacuum. A literature review acts as a solid background for a research study. All researchers emphasize on this part as it's an account of what has already been known about a particular phenomenon. It also determines the gaps and inconsistencies present in the existing studies. For this study too an extensive review of literature has been done from various sources. This chapter reviews the existing studies influencing adolescents' role in family purchase decisions and an attempt has been made to fill the gap present in the already done research or studies.

"Expressive" aspects of consumption have been developed due to peer communication. In this, the influence of parents and peers as socialization agents has been investigated, along with the effects of demographic variables on materialism among adolescents (Moschis and Moore, 1978).

Family, school, peers and mass media have a significant impact on consumer skills and effectiveness of existing consumer education material and practices. Older adolescents are able to manage finance better than younger ones and have socially more desirable behaviour. Male adolescents are more aware about consumer matters than female counterparts (Moschis and Churchill, 1978).

Family communication has a vital role in adolescents' consumer learning and in determining the importance of the various mechanisms such as social interaction, modelling and reinforcement, through which such learning occurs. Protective families, where ultimate decisions are taken by parents, are more likely to have negative reinforcement. Consensual families are where parents take decisions but adolescents are given the opportunity to give their opinion, with parents explaining their eventual decisions (Moschis et al., 1984a).

Various family patterns have different attitudes towards the market. Adolescents belonging to laissez-faire families are less likely to have brand preferences, and are not much different from adolescents from pluralistic families who have a negative attitude towards the marketplace. On the other hand, consensual adolescents are more likely to have a positive attitude towards the marketplace and are not satisfied with the products they buy or use (Moschis *et al.*, 1986).

A significant relationship has been found between market knowledge of adolescents and the mothers' and teachers' role model influence. Similarly, a positive relationship exists between adolescents' market knowledge and athletes' and entertainers' role model influence but there was not any such relationship between the fathers' role model influence and adolescents' market knowledge (Clark *et al.*, 2001).

Parents and TV advertisements have a part to play in consumer socialization of young adolescents. It was concluded that parents' efforts to socialize young adolescents by using TV advertisements are not highly valued (North and Kotzé, 2001). The internet was found to be negatively related in socializing them. Older adolescents and those belonging to a high economic class were found to be less reserved (Moscardelli and Liston-Heyes, 2005).

It is evident that adolescents become more materialistic when they are under stress because of their parents' divorce. Family structure affects compulsive buying in the case of older adolescents, whereas there is no such relation in the case of younger adolescents (Roberts *et al.*, 2003, 2006). Peers are positive predictors of materialistic consumption values while advertising is not a significant predictor. The main objective here was examining the influence of peers, media celebrities and advertisements on adolescents' materialistic values (La Ferle and Chan, 2008).

Adolescents' and parents' interaction for TV advertisements acts as a consumer socialization agent and, thus, the impact of advertisements on the buying decisions of adolescents. It has been concluded that age and gender of adolescents impacts the interaction with their parents relating to TV advertisements as well as the way they observe them (Ozmete, 2009). Sometimes, materialistic parents as well as peers are also materialistic (Chaplin and John, 2010).

Secondary school students have a positive attitude towards consumer education and the majority of them apply it to a great extent in the market, but, because of inadequate facilities, consumer education is sparse (Ukpore, 2010). Communication with peers and alcohol advertising favoured alcohol consumption and positively influenced brand recall in the case of younger individuals (15 to 17 year olds). In the case of adults (individuals between the ages of 18 and 25 years), alcohol consumption was found to be determined by brand recall (Manuel Sancho *et al.*, 2011).

Cultural differences were found among customers in assessing luxury value dimensions. It was found that Iranian customers believed that high price means high quality. Also, quality value and usability had impact on the evaluation of luxury goods. "Conspicuous" value has been found as the most important dimension for customers in Iran. The study provided empirical evidence on Iranian consumption behaviour from the Muslim point of view (Teimourpour and Heidarzadeh Hanzaee, 2011). Socio-oriented family communication structure may stimulate materialism among young people whereas concept-oriented family communication has no effect on the development of materialism among young adults (Moschis *et al.*, 2011).

Adolescents who use media, and feel less maternal care, are more likely to consume (Gudmunson and Beutler, 2012). Less consumer awareness was found in residents of suburban areas as compared to urban area residents (Ishak and Zabil, 2012). Customer socialization agents have an influence on branded apparel purchase among tweens (Boon *et al.*, 2013).

Media makes children susceptible to the external environment by generating materialism. This materialism leads to excessive consumption and impulsive purchasing by young customers. Parents need to divert a child's attention from the materialistic to the real world. Hence, a parent's guidance is very significant in reducing the effect of materialism among children (Vandana and Lenka, 2014).

Impoverished and affluent children have materialistic values. Materialism was also found between younger children (ages 8–10 years) from poor families and affluent families. At age 11–13 years and beyond (ages 16–17 years) children and adolescents from impoverished families were more materialistic than their wealthier counterparts (Chaplin *et al.*, 2014). People who were highly susceptible to reference groups, have a high level of prestige sensitivity. Also, they were more materialistic and more likely to engage in status consumption (Kim and Jang, 2014).

Advertisements create positive images of brands and products in the minds of children leading to purchase requests by them. Parents developed a customer culture in children. Parents, peers, the internet and TV were found to be strong sources of influence for customer socialization of children (Estrela *et al.*, 2014). Customer knowledge led to better selection of credit cards. Despite being more knowledgeable, young professionals were more likely to select a credit card based on impulse as compared to college students (Cakarnis and D'Alessandro, 2015).

Chinese adolescents do not endorse materialistic values. Moreover, younger adolescents had lower level of materialistic values as compared to older ones. Parental rejection was found to significantly affect adolescents' materialistic values (Fu *et al.*, 2015). Adolescents' involvement with reality TV resulted in consumer socialization through values and attitudes related to consumption (Haq and Rahman, 2015). There is a boost in materialism due to exposure to advertising significantly influencing the quality of life of customers. Material possessions would enhance their social positions. Adolescents gave little time to their family and relationships (Sandhu, 2015).

2.1 Factors Influencing Customer Socialization of Adolescents

Learning of advertising slogans is mainly a function of the intelligence of adolescents. Adolescents' customer learning is not simply an individual stimulus response phenomenon, but is a social learning process. It may be fruitful to think of media advertising as shaping the content and form of interpersonal perceptions and communication, rather than considering the media as dispensers of product information (Ward and Wackman, 1971).

Adolescents observe the consumption behaviour of their parents: they hear that parents discuss expenses and see which products are bought and used. Parents act as a role model for their adolescents. Parents influence the degree to which adolescents achieve customer knowledge through the type, quantity and quantity of customer experiences which they share with them. Adolescents' skills to handle money increased, as they grew older. There isn't a significant relationship between exposure to TV commercials and adolescents' customer learning (Ward, 1977).

TV viewing and, consequently, the number of TV advertisements to which adolescents are exposed, predicts their social motivations for consumption and materialistic attitudes. More exposure to the medium may lead to learning the "expressive" aspects of consumption. The family was reported teaching "rational" aspects of consumption to adolescents. Peer influence also seems to be an important socialization agent to the learning of materialistic values by adolescents (Moschis and Churchill, 1978).

Information source preferences vary according to type of product. Parents were preferred as a source of information for products where price, social acceptance and performances are of great concern (wristwatch, dress shoes, pocket calculator and hair dryer). Peers were recognized as important in buying decisions concerning items important for peer acceptance, like sunglasses and wallets, while mass media ranks relatively low and preferred for items where price and performance were of little concern (flash cubes and household batteries) (Moschis and Moore, 1979).

The amount of TV viewing was shown to function as a mediating variable between demographic variables income and education and affluence estimates. Heavy soap opera viewers constructed their estimates significantly faster than light viewers, which suggests that relevant information is more accessible in memory for heavy viewers than light viewers (O'Guinn and Shrum, 1997).

Adolescents of all ages receive an allowance but it is more likely to be given to adolescents of 11 years and above. Street merchants were also preferred by adolescents with department stores least popular. Adolescents who are frequently taken by their parents to the marketplace as co-purchasers soon develop independent purchasing behaviour (McNeal and Hwa Yeh, 1997).

The major customer socialization factors influence adolescents' purchase behaviours – irrational social influence, importance of TV, familial influence, shopping importance and brand importance – then were used as dependent variables in subsequent analyses looking at the effects of a number of independent variables. The relative impacts of the various customer socialization influence/factors do vary according to the adolescent's gender, age, amount of spending money available, amount of TV viewing and how he/she spends time after school (Dotson and Hyatt, 2005).

Parents engage in customer behaviour instructions through both direct and indirect means. Direct customer learning is intentional instructions by the parent for the purpose of teaching the adolescent some aspects of customer learning, while indirect learning is the unintentional instruction of some aspects of customer behaviour that is initiated by the adolescent through direct observation or participation. Parents place adolescents in a customer situation, as in many situations parents and adolescents are together when the activity takes place – often referred to co-shopping. However, parents' socialization behaviour seems to be most related to the individual characteristics of the adolescent, as parents are most restrictive and make more decisions for younger adolescents than older adolescents. The family's socio-economic status also appears to play a role in customer socialization (Chan, 2008).

Rural adolescents perceived personal sources to be more useful as well as more credible than commercial sources in obtaining information about new products and services. Older adolescents found parents and grand-parents less useful and less credible than did younger adolescents for new product information. However, older adolescents did not find peers more useful and credible than younger adolescents (Chan and McNeal, 2006).

Mostly adolescents spent the money immediately or after just saving only enough to buy a desired item; others preferred to save their money for the sake of saving it or for a specific future endeavour. Money was spent mainly on food, toys and clothes; sometimes on the impulse of the moment and associated with later guilt. TV was considered a big source of information on new products, but regarded as untrustworthy. When they could not get what they wanted, most adolescents appealed to negotiation strategies; many also reported feeling sad or upset (Fiates *et al.*, 2008).

Peers have an important influence during adolescence and marketing action should reflect this influence. Promotions for products intended for teenagers' use (e.g. clothing) may be more convincing if the presentation shows a teenage accompanied by peers because, during adolescence, teenagers express a need to identify themselves with peers. The relevance of a product to a teenager may be strengthened or validated by communication and interaction with peers about that product (Aoud and Neeley, 2008).

2.2 Adolescents' Exposure to Media

Media exposure reflected a range of cognitive and affective reactions towards TV commercials. For convenience in the literature review, the items were abbreviated as TRUTH, ANNOY, GOODONLY, LIKE, PERSUADE, BELIEVE and BESTBUY. The first three items out of seven describe the credibility dimension, two items the likeability of commercials and the last two the persuasive power of TV advertising. The adolescents showed a negative attitude towards TV commercials (Rossiter, 1977).

For boys, new video media were associated with higher reports of arousal and more positive affective states than was the case for the activities of TV viewing, reading and listening to popular music. Relative to boys, girls reported lower affect and arousal, especially during video games and music videos (Kubey and Larson, 1990). Western adolescents have access to TV sets or a video recorder in their own room. Some of them have greater access to computers in their homes and are much more likely to have internet links (van der Voort *et al.*, 1998).

TV undoubtedly still occupies a dominant position in the lives of adolescents and teenagers in all countries. With regard to personal computer and TV related games, availability and amount of use differ considerably, with Swedish young people being ahead of those in Flanders and Germany (Johnsson-Smaragdi *et al.*, 1998). Most households contain most media (computers and video game systems are the exception); the majority of youth have their own personal media. The average youth devotes 6¾ hours to media a day; simultaneous use of multiple media increases exposure to 8 hours of media messages daily. Overall, media exposure and exposure to individual media vary as a function of age, gender, race/ethnicity and family socio-economic level. TV remains the dominant medium. About one-half of the youth sampled use a computer daily. A substantial proportion of adolescents' media use occurs in the absence of parents (Roberts, 2000).

Boys are more likely than girls to have a TV in their own room, and content preferences are dramatically different. The mother's educational status is directly related to patterns of electronic media use rather than father's, and adolescents' commitment to school has been shown to predict music preferences (Roe, 2000).

Adolescents' internet usage continues to increase, with most saying they used the internet and social media for a couple of years, with an average of 5 to 10 hours' time spent online for medium users (Clarke, 2002). The mobile phone is, for adolescents, a medium which permits communication without the surveillance of parents, families and teachers. Other uses of the mobile in addition to chatting and making arrangements, although not always positive, were also made apparent. Pupils claimed to have spent money on their mobile calls every month as well as their on purchasing the mobile and its up-keep (Davie *et al.*, 2004). Adolescents had access to and used mobile and cordless phones early in life and there was a rapid increase in use with age. Girls generally reported more frequent use than boys (Soderqvist *et al.*, 2007).

Household ownership of new media, ownership of a mobile phone and heavy use of the internet were more prevalent among Danish tweens than among Hong Kong tweens. Danish tweens were more likely to use mobile phones and the internet for interpersonal communication and for enjoyment than Hong Kong tweens. Hong Kong tweens used the internet more for educational purposes than Danish tween (Andersen *et al.*, 2007).

The internet is mainly used for listening to music and for fun. The internet was the preferred media choice for information-driven activities. Magazines retained importance for entertainment and shopping activities while TV retained importance for new and current affairs. Most of the respondents found useful websites through search engines: interpersonal information sources gave way to the internet for obtaining information about sensitive issues (Chan and Fang, 2007).

Adolescents in urban areas used media such as TV, the internet and computer games, and rural–urban residency had the most significant craze for TV viewing. Besides, parents of urban adolescents had concerns about media usage, whereas a greater proportion of adolescents in rural areas had TVs in their bedrooms and ate meals while watching TV (Davey, 2008).

Girls used the internet far more often for social activities such as chatting and e-mail while boys preferred to use it for entertainment and computational activities, such as gaming, e-commerce, viewing multimedia and for programming. Girls used their mobile phones far more often for text messaging (Short Message Service – SMS) than boys, who more frequently used their mobile phones for technical functions (alarm, gaming, internet, etc.) There was no gender gap in everyday phone usage (Watten *et al.*, 2008).

Four significant predictors of screen media time usage (SMTU) emerged. First, the type of school was associated with the media of our study, particularly students from state/public school spent more time on social media than their private school counterparts. Second, older adolescents (14–16 years old) were more likely to use computer/videogames and a mobile phone. Boys spent significantly more time on a mobile phone than girls. Additionally, adolescents seemed to consume more TV and computer/videogames in autumn than in winter and more TV and mobile phones on weekends than on weekdays (Devís Devís *et al.*, 2009).

Students in Finland consider the specific features "clock", "phone", "high battery life", "alarm" and "calendar" as very important, and the specific features "TV connectivity", "joystick", "live TV", "Twitter" and "small screen size" as unimportant features. There were also significant differences in the specific feature preferences among high school, undergraduate and graduate students. In addition, there were differences in the way the respondents conceptualized the specific feature preferences of the cell phone (Haverilla, 2012).

2.3 TV as a Major Contributor in Media

Premium format commercials were more effective than host and announcer commercials in producing desired behaviour. Premium TV advertising influenced adolescents' attitudes and behaviour. But it did not consider the impact of various other variables such as the amount of TV viewing, family income, adolescents' IQ level and attitude towards TV commercials (Miller and Busch, 1979).

There is a considerable difference between adolescents' attitude and adults' attitude towards TV advertisements. Adolescents view TV advertisements almost entirely in terms of their entertainment function. Their purchase behaviour may not be manipulated by such advertisement. They found two reasons for this: (1) their perception of these advertisements may not be consistent with the advertisers' primary intentions; and (2) they are less entertained and more irritated and bored with such advertisements as they grow old (Barling and Fullagar, 1983). The least common approaches used to promote products were safety/quality of material and peer status and popularity (Kunkel, 1992).

Humour is a common practice in advertising and synthesis of the current literature led to several conclusions. Some of them are: (1) humour attracts attention; (2) customer non-durables are best suited to humour treatment; (3) soft drinks and snack foods are best suited to humour; (4) humour enhances liking, in fact the link between humour and liking is stronger than for any other factors; (5) the nature of the product affects the appropriateness of a humour treatment (Weinberger and Gulas, 1992).

There exists a conflict between appreciation of the personal uses and economic value of advertising and appreciation of cultural degradation. The reason for this conflict was, first, because of factors such as age, family responsibilities, lifestyles, media availability and, second, beliefs interact with preferences and value system to determine overall dispositions between two populations (Pollay and Mittal, 1993). Adolescents have more liking towards advertisements. They tended to enjoy the advertisements they saw, and found them more informative and useful in guiding their own decision making. They tended to feel more confident in advertising claims when they went for their actual purchase decisions (Shavitt *et al.*, 1998).

The most typical appeals in commercials aimed at male adolescents were action-adventures, sports and play, whereas commercials aimed at female adolescents emphasized nurturing, physical attractiveness, friendship and romance. Having the best, competition and achievement were the dominant appeals in commercials aimed at male teenagers, whereas romance, sexuality and belonging to a group were emphasized in commercials aimed at female teenagers. Appeals with regard to product categories were humour, quality, fun and newness which were prevalent in every product category. In contrast, appeals such as play, pleasant taste, health and safety seem to be more specially associated with toys, food products, personal care products and cars, respectively (Buijzen and Valkenburg, 2002).

As the attempts made in the past (Rossiter, 1977) to assess adolescents' attitude towards TV advertising dated back to 20 years ago, a new investigation of adolescents' advertising attitude seems absolutely necessary. Thus, a new scale measuring general attitudes towards TV advertising has been developed (Derbaix and Pecheux, 2003).

Adolescents' attitude towards TV advertising was measured, focusing on the range of cognitive and affective reactions towards TV advertising in terms of perceived truthfulness and potential annoying qualities. Adolescents' attitude towards advertising was the main predictor on purchase of goods. The more positive attitude, the more influence they make on parent purchase (Ghani and Zain, 2004).

Adolescents perceive half of the TV commercials to be true, although this varies by grade and geography. Adolescents in Beijing perceived TV commercials to be more trustworthy than did adolescents in Nanjing and Chengdu. The percentage of adolescents who perceive all commercials to be true declines consistently with grade. Adolescents in higher grades depend more on brand and user experience, while adolescents in lower grades hold both a strong liking and disliking for commercials. These strong feelings towards advertising decreased with grade, being replaced by a marked increase in neutral or indifferent feelings. Perceived truthfulness of TV advertising is related positively with liking for a commercial (Chan and McNeal, 2004).

Adolescents are more positive about advertising as an institution than the instruments used to promote advertising. While product information acquisition is the main personal use of advertising which influences general attitudes to advertising in Bulgaria, the entertaining value of advertising was found the strongest personal use in Romania (Petrovici and Marinov, 2005).

Music advertisements were a more effective stimulus of attention and memory than advertising without popular music. Popular music clearly has attention elements attached to brand name recalling. It also has the ability to enhance memory for the brand. However, the effects of significant songs and artists on brand memory were observed for one of the brands (Long) and the artist Eminem, and showed men were more sensitive to the level of personal significance they have for an advertising message integrated in popular music than females (Allan, 2006).

Mothers thought that premiums involving collectables were particularly influential in driving demand for food products such as sweet cereals, chips and fast food. Mothers also noted that their adolescents associate "fun" with premiums and, subsequently, the brand. However, fun was also associated with products themselves, as distinct from the premium (participants said that their adolescents play with fun foods by dunking (Dunkaroos), unwinding (Roll-ups) and shredding (Cheese Strings) (Pettigrew and Roberts, 2006).

The most frequently used promotional strategies were the use of jingles/ slogans, showing adolescents the food, and the use of product identification characters. The use of animation, real adolescents, animals with human characteristics, fast-cutting scenes, exciting fast-paced music, humour and colour effects were the most used attention elements in the commercials (Page and Brewster, 2007).

To beat the clutter and break the ice, companies are increasingly using humour in their advertisements as it forces the audience to watch, laugh, enjoy and, most importantly, helps the audience to recall the brand. Humorous advertisements have better and easier recall because they elevate customers' happiness and moods. Humour can be deployed in various ways, including using a comedian, capitalizing on current topics and strong idea-based humour, which requires low investments and emphasis on purchases and those advertisements have to explain the benefits of products to customers. Now many advertisers are using a comedian to introduce humour in advertisements as leading brand Domino's pizza has recently taken the services of Paresh Rawal to be successful (Ganapatthy, 2009).

Companies are using games, particularly computer games or video games such as the "power of pepsi men", American Army and Urban Jungle, through which players are exposed to a company's brands and attempts are made to turn the players into customers. Several companies like ICICI prudential life insurance, airtel, are using games for advertising their products (Prabhi, 2009).

The animation industry in India is growing at a rapid pace. The major reasons for this tremendous growth in the animated industry were: (1) availability of high tech animated studios, supported by necessary hardware, software and communication infrastructure; (2) an increase of demand in animation in advertising industry due to (a) dynamic medium that uses motion to tell a story or to create an appeal, (b) lesser TV airtime is consumed as lengthy messages can be packed into shorter time, (c) the most famous AIDAS (A-attention, I-interest, D-desire, A-action, S-satisfaction) theory fits in animated advertisements as viewers get attracted towards them naturally (Maheshwari, 2009).

Adolescents' attitudes towards TV advertising are measured on three dimensions – credence, enjoyment and purchase-intention – as well as demonstrating its psychometric reliability and validity. A self-report measure of adolescents' attitudes towards TV advertising is described. The credence of TV advertising decreases significantly according to age groups (D'Alessio *et al.*, 2009).

The more negative the attitudes to TV advertisements, the greater the intensity of TV advertisements avoidance and vice versa. Advertisers should consider that advertisements avoidance is a real fact which cannot be ignored. Therefore, they must take this avoidance into consideration in planning and executing advertising campaigns (El-Adly, 2010). There exists a positive relationship between celebrity endorsements and purchase intentions as celebrity endorsement, both single and multiple, creates a positive attitude towards advertisements and positive attitude towards the brand (Pandey, 2010). Role model endorsers have a positive influence on young adults' product switching behaviour, complaint behaviour, positive word of mouth behaviour and brand loyalty. This confirms the assumption that sports celebrities are important socialization agents and can have a significant impact on purchase behaviours and intention of young customers (Dix and Pougnet, 2010).

Promotional characters, celebrity endorsers and premium offers were used more frequently to promote non-core than core foods, even on dedicated adolescents' channels. Brand equity characters featured on a greater proportion of food adverts than licensed characters. This extensive analysis of TV adverts demonstrated that the use of persuasive marketing techniques to promote unhealthy foods was extensive in broadcasting popular advertisements with adolescents, despite regulations (Boyland *et al.*, 2011).

2.4 Adolescents' Influence in Family Purchase Decisions

Adolescents frequently attempt to influence purchases for food products, but these attempts decreased with age. Durables used by adolescents were the second most requested products category. However, for all categories purchase attempts decrease with age (Ward and Wackman, 1972). Adolescents exerted minimal influence in the major decision categories, i.e. prices of furniture, major appliances, automobiles, groceries, family saving and insurance decisions, however they have a high influence in vacation decisions (Jenkins, 1979).

Adolescents tend to have more say in the purchase of products that are rather expensive and for their own use. Additionally compared to parents' ratings, adolescents appeared to overstate their relative influence. Due to dual earnings, family income is increasing and it is not surprising that parents at least perceive themselves to have greater influence in purchasing matters than their adolescents do. Several factors like older father, a concept-oriented family communication style, fewer adolescents and mothers who worked fewer hours outside the home were found responsible for increased adolescents' influence in family purchases (Foxman *et al.*, 1989).

Parents' dual income status allows adolescents greater influence in some family durable purchases, but this does not affect self-purchases where their influence is already substantial. These effects are pronounced for products that teens care for (e.g. stereo) and use often (e.g. telephone). Parents' dual income status seems to allow teens greater influence for some durable family purchases (Beatty and Talpade, 1994).

Adolescents' purchase influence might vary under different types of families. The family type and family authority relationships influence adolescents' purchase decisions (Mangleburg *et al.*, 1999). Adolescents in single parent families had a greater influence on both types of product decisions as compared to adolescents in step-families and intact families as they are subject to less parental coalition formation and authoritarianism in parent–adolescent relations which, in turn, enhances their influence in purchase decisions (Larkin, 1977). Step-parents have a less positive effect towards adolescents than original parents do.

In the new urban Indian family, adolescents were influencers/ co-deciders at the time of purchase of personal products, consumables, financial products, vacations, educational products and family automobiles while they were buyers of family toiletries and initiators or gatekeepers for purchases of household durables (Dhobal, 1999). Adolescents whose parents are perceived as using a more conceptual style and/or a social style of communication tend to show a higher level of participation in discussion. This participation appears to represent an opportunity for parents to encourage their teenagers, whatever their style, to develop as customers (Lachance *et al.*, 2000).

The initiator for purchase in a family was typically a young female member, who was likely to be the wife or one of the adolescents. As influencers, younger members, especially adolescents, were found to affect purchase of a personal computer, audio system and TV. The final purchases were found to be decided upon after consultation with other family members, mainly the husband. Adolescents have not been observed to have a large impact on instrumental decisions such as how much to spend, but rather play a role while making expressive decisions such as colour, model, brand, shape, at the time of purchase (Kapoor, 2001).

Product selection decisions in rural families were mostly made by spouses together but they were highly influenced by adolescents. Further, the brand selection decisions were also made jointly by the couple but were importantly influenced by adolescents in the family. The store where the durables were purchased as well as the making of the actual purchase decision was also made jointly or by the husband individually (for the durables, but not for air coolers). However, adolescents also "went to buy", that is accompanied their parents at the time of buying, TVs, washing machines and refrigerators (Hundal, 2001). Younger adolescents whose mothers are housewives have more influence than younger adolescents whose mothers work for "just a job" or career (Lee and Beatty, 2002). Fathers had the highest influence for the final decision for TV and car, as compared to vacations, appliances, furniture and cereal products, where the parents had a higher influence than their teenage adolescents. However, product category, the decision phase and the decision aspects vary (Shoham and Dalakas, 2003).

Adolescents in different regions are very similar in regard to the product categories that they had the highest influence in. They are also similar in regard to the product categories with the lowest influences, on family car and living room furniture in both cases. The pattern of adolescents' general influence on buying facets was also consistent (Shoham and Dalakas, 2005). Adolescents from blended families have less say in family purchase decisions as parents did not want to increase the compulsivity of purchase by giving their adolescents a say in discussions and final outcome (Tinson *et al.*, 2008). Parents considered that three areas where adolescents had the most influence were shopping with parents, suggesting a brand and drawing attention to new products. Parents perceived that the influence of boys was stronger than the influence of girls on decision making of all specific products (Sener, 2011).

2.5 Parent–Adolescent Conflict Resolving Strategies

The problem solving tactics of information search, family discussion, delegation to the most knowledgeable member, were most often used for all products (that is, vacation, appliance, furniture) except breakfast cereal, where persuasion tactics of exertion of authority were used. Bargaining tactics of promising future considerations and delaying of decision were rarely used across all product categories. The use of the persuasion tactic of coalition between two or more family members was also relatively low (Belch *et al.*, 1985). Bargaining was the most common strategy adopted by adolescents when trying to influence the purchase of products for personal use. Conflict avoidance was most commonly used for family use products. However, for products for home use, such as a personal computer, they resorted to problem solving tactics to resolve conflicts (Johnson, 1995). While bargaining is most common in dyadic interactions (Qualls, 1982), problem solving is more frequent in triadic interactions between mother, father and adolescent.

Adolescents adopt five dimensions of influence, namely, persuasion, not eating, acting stubbornly, approaching the other parent and playing on emotion (Palan and Wilkes, 1997). Adolescents have a variety of influence strategies including bargaining strategies, promotional strategies, emotional strategies, request strategies, expert strategies, expert strategies and legitimate strategies to influence the outcome of family purchasing decisions. They are especially likely to use bargaining money deals, other deals, reasons and persuasion as strategies to influence decision outcomes (Palan and Wilkes, 1997). Adolescents' direct influence attempt scales were shown to be significantly related to (yet distinct from) the Narcissistic Personality Inventory's (Raskin and Hall, 1979; Raskin and Terry, 1988) entitlement and the social power scales reward, coercion and legitimacy (Williams and Burns, 2000).

Advertisers are the first to recognize adolescents' value as customers who are capable of making decisions about spending. They have become active participants in the family purchase decisions. Not only do adolescents have their "own money" to spend on a variety of products and services of their own choice, they also have extensive influence on how their parents buy products and services. Adolescents' influence tactics include eliciting the desired parental purchasing behaviour by: pressurizing tactics, upward appeal, exchange tactics, coalition tactics, ingratiating tactics, rational persuasion, inspirational appeals and consultation tactics (Wimalasire, 2004).

2.6 Parents' Attitude and Perception Towards TV Advertisements

Parents may embrace both positive and negative mediation strategies, one or neither. Positive mediation may occur more due to happenstance, while negative mediation is associated more often with critical viewing and protective motivations (Austin *et al.*, 1999).

Parents of younger adolescents were more critical than parents of older adolescents as they were worried about adolescents' inability to identify misleading content in commercials. Parents who have more negative attitudes towards advertising exercise their control through coercion, rather than through communication (Chan and McNeal, 2002). Advertisements lead adolescents to pressurize their parents to buy them things; the more advertisements adolescents watch, the more they want advertised products and advertisements persuade them to buy products they do not really need (Young *et al.*, 2003).

TV commercials lead to an increase in number of requests for advertised products which also increases the number of product denials because parents cannot honour all requests made by their adolescents. This makes the adolescent unhappy. This may also be because when an adolescent watches an advertisement, he or she compares his/her situation with the idealized world in the commercials and the gap between the two makes him unhappy. Parent–adolescent customer communication and parental mediation of advertising are important moderators of the effects of advertising on adolescents' purchase requests and materialism (Buijzen and Valkenburg, 2003).

Due to the constant exposure of adolescents to TV advertisements, they are able to differentiate between good and bad products and are in the situation to convince their parents easily to purchase the product they desire (Wilson and Wood, 2004).

Parents do have reservations about advertising to adolescents but at the same time accepted it as fact of life in a customer society. Parents recognize their own responsibility to educate their adolescents as the statement goes: "It's up to parents to explain to adolescents that they cannot have everything they see advertised". A particular negative potential effect of adolescents' advertising is the "pester power" or "nag factor", i.e. "advertising encourages adolescents' to nag their parents into something that is not good for them, they don't need or the parents cannot afford" (Spungin, 2004).

Family conflicts and pestering are among the most important drivers of restrictive mediation of TV. Attitudes towards food advertising, the degree to which adolescents' can understand the commercial intent of advertising and the perceived influence of advertisements on adolescents do not directly affect restrictive mediation (Dens *et al.*, 2007). TV advertisements are an important factor which drives adolescents' product choice and inculcate unhealthy eating habits in them. Indian adolescents love watching TV and prefer it over social interaction, physical and development activities. TV advertisements provide adolescents with knowledge about products and brands. Adolescents demand more of the product of which advertisements they like (Mittal *et al.*, 2010).

2.7 Role of Socio-economic Factors and Communication Pattern

Child-centred mothers were more likely to be influenced by their children and family-oriented mothers or women with close knit families were more sensitive to children's influence. Mothers co-viewing TV programmes with their children were more likely to yield to children's influencing attempt for products advertised on those shows (Mehrotra and Torges, 1977). Children do tend to make forceful demands at the point of purchase: their success depends on whether they "ask" or "tell" (Atkin, 1978).

Customer socialization of adolescents includes many different elements, such as age, family communication structure, co-shopping and advertisements/mass media. Customer socialization also influences the development of brand preferences, as well as materialistic tendencies. "Customer socialization is the process by which young people acquire skills, knowledge and attitude relevant to their functioning in the marketplace" (Carlson and Grossbart, 1988). In other words, customer socialization is how adolescents learn to be customers. Adolescents spend most of the time with their family members and, thus, family is the most influential agent of socialization. The roles of husbands, wives and children vary across stages of decision making. They found that while the role of the teenage child was most prominent at the initiation stage, it was limited thereafter (Belch *et al.*, 1985). Subsequently, Foxman *et al.* (1989a, 1989b) reported more evidence supporting discrepancies in reports.

A child in a single parent family, higher socio-economic status and higher personal resources and in a sex role egalitarian family will have more influence. A child will have greater influence for product purchase decisions that he/she considers important or for which he/she has high product knowledge. A child's participation in family decision making will tend to increase his/her satisfaction with family purchase decisions (Leistritz *et al.*, 1987).

Children of engineers and doctors were found to have remarkable influence in purchase decisions. The influence of the child varied across several parameters such as product, the age of the child and the sex role orientation of the mother (Ahuja and Stinson, 1993). It is commonly expected that advertising effects will be diluted when customers encounter advertisements for competing brands. Consequently, advertisers attempt to avoid competitors' advertisements when buying media. Advertising for mature and familiar brands may not work in the same way as advertising for unfamiliar brands. Relative to information related to the more familiar brands advertised in the marketplace, they may be less susceptible to competitive inference (Mayer, 1994).

Adolescents have considerable influence in making purchases and concluded that, besides products for direct consumption, children display influence in purchasing products for family consumption where parents are less involved and perceive little or no product differentiation (for food products) (Jensen, 1995). Adolescents do influence family decisions and this influence may vary across different factors. For example, adolescents have greater influence in household purchasing decisions in a concept-oriented communication environment (in which children are encouraged to develop their own ideas) and when their personal sources are greater (Palan and Wilkes, 1997).

The shift in influence of adolescents has occurred as a result of families having fewer children, more dual-income couples who can afford to permit their children to make a greater number of choices and encouragement by the media to allow children to "express themselves". Still further single parent households often push their children towards household participation and self-reliance (Schiffman, 1997).

Adolescents' attitude towards a particular brand is more crucial to understand than their choice behaviour and this is important not only to understand their customer behaviour as children but also their future behaviour as adults (Palan and Wilkes, 1997).

Children in the perceptual stage (3–7 years) focus on perceptually salient features of products and use direct requests and emotional appeals to influence purchases, and possess limited ability to adapt strategy to a person or a situation. They are expedient in making decisions, are egocentric and have the emerging ability to adapt to cost–benefit trade-offs. However, children in the analytical stage (7–11 years) are more thoughtful, focus on important attribute information to generate an expanded repertoire of strategies (especially non-compensatory ones) and are capable of adapting strategies to tasks. In the reflective stage (11–16 years), children have substantial brand awareness for adult-oriented as well as child-oriented product categories, possess ability to gather information on functional, perceptual and social aspects, and are capable of adapting strategies to tasks in an adult-like manner (John, 1999).

There are changes in the role of children for making buying decisions in different product categories. Children now act as influencers/co-deciders for personal products, for vacations and for consumables, whereas they are buyers for family toiletries, initiator/gatekeeper for household durables and co-deciders/users for family automobiles, financial products and vacations (Dhobhal, 1999).

When there is a conflict in more than two family members during the purchase decision processes then the third parties (children) may form an alliance to aid one side against the other. At the same time, the influence of family members varies in response to the gender mix of the children. Daughters were generally more influential than sons and the gender of elder children appeared to have more significance on the influence structure of the family than that of younger children. Interestingly, fathers and elder daughters, and mothers and sons, were found to work together to gain influence. The influence of a mother in the family was the strongest during the Negotiation and Outcome stage when both her children were male. Her influence was also strong if her first child was male and the second child was a female. The mother–son and father–daughter pattern changed when parents had two daughters. The father had less influence during the Configuration stage when he had a younger daughter and his influence increased in the Outcome stage if the couple had an elder daughter and a younger son. Moreover, mothers in two-girl families had greater decision powers than when the family has an elder daughter and a younger son (Lee and Collins, 1999).

An adolescent is often the most advertising savvy person in the entire household. International manufacturers of packaged foods have gone beyond merely making the product accessible and attractive to adolescents. Now, the mantra is "sell to the adolescent and close with the parent". Marketers must gain an intimate understanding of a child's emotional needs, their hopes and fantasies in order to succeed in creating and sustaining bonds with almost universal child appeal (Vecchio, 2000).

When children feel entitled or privileged to act in their own way, they resort to negative influence attempts such as deception, displaying anger, begging or pleading to exert influence. If they find that their parents have the right or legitimate power to direct their actions, they utilize positive influence attempts such as asking nicely, showing affection or bargaining. When they feel that they can manipulate their parents, they try to deceive the parents, display anger, or beg and plead. If the children expect to be punished as a result of non-compliance, they behave in ways that are perceived as positive by parents. When parents resort to coercive tactics, children try to get their own way by asking nicely, bargaining or showing affection. Many times children also express compliance in exchange for a future gain; that is, they bargain for a future reward in exchange for a present one (Williams and Burns, 2000). Individual family members were associated with multiple roles, such as the initiator for a purchase in a family was typically a young female member, who was likely to be the wife or one of the children. As influencers, younger members, especially children, were found to affect the purchase of a personal computer, audio system and TV. The final purchases were found to be decided upon after consultation with other family members, mainly the husband (Kapoor, 2001).

Adolescents have a lot of information because of exposure to TV, other media and friends. They reflected that parents sought their opinion even in purchasing products not directly related to the children, such as cars, because of their higher knowledge of brands, models and the latest trends. Also, children stated that parents bought products that made the kids happy (Halan, 2002). Children are also major targets for TV advertising, whose impact is greater than usual because there is an apparent lessening of influence by parents and others in the older generation. Nevertheless, $1 billion a year is spent on advertisements and commercials directed at children (Shah, 2003).

Adolescents today do not only make their buying decisions themselves but also play a great role in other buying decisions of the products to be purchased in the household. They not only attempt to influence their parents to make purchases of special interest to them, but also with regard to remote interest, e.g. laundry detergents, for which they see advertisements on TV. Thus this segment can very well be exploited in order to peep into parents' mind (Singh and Kumar, 2003). Levy (1996) discusses the family dinner as an aspiration for everyday family unity and virtue: "The ideal vision is of the family members coming together every evening from their diverse and separate activities to affirm their relatedness and love" (p. 324). Today, separations, divorces, co-habitation, remarriages, single parent families, homosexual partnerships, extramarital affairs, remaining singles, flings etc. are reality in the Western world. Even so, the nuclear family is often presented in advertising. The essence of every family is co-operation (Leistritz *et al.*, 1987).

Adolescents perceived their role to be highly important in the family's decisions. They play the role of influencer and decider in the purchase of a majority of personal products, consumables, household durables and even family automobiles. They also play the role of buyer for a number of products (Verma and Kapoor, 2004). Adolescents are individually active in initiating the idea to purchase a durable. In other stages of the decision making process, they exhibit joint influence along with other members of the family. This implies that they provide support to the member exerting influence to increase pressure but do not wield much influence individually (Kaur and Singh, 2004).

Teens who perceive themselves to be internet mavens (individuals who are relied upon more for providing information from the virtual market-place) as well as their parents, believed that teens were more influential in all stages – initiation and information search, alternative evaluation and final decision stages. However, their influence was higher in the initiation and information search stages as compared to alternative evaluation and final decision stages (Belch *et al.*, 1985).

Indian society vastly differs from the West in terms of family composition and structure, values, norms and behaviour which affect the role that children play in purchase decision making in the household sector. Western researchers have taken into account the effect of family type and composition, sex role orientation, parent style etc. to bring out a complete picture regarding the role of children: Indian literature is more limited in this regard. Indian authors have gauged the influence of children only partially and have generally focused on spouses or all family members. So, research especially centred on children is needed (Singh and Kaur, 2006). With an increase in the age of the child, cognitive understanding of advertisements increased and children above the age of 8 years were able to respond to TV advertisements in a mature and informed manner. Heavy viewing was positively associated with favourable attitudes towards TV advertisements and, conversely, interest in advertisements decline with age. Children's exposure to TV advertisements was determined to a large extent by parents' control of their viewing. Parent–child interaction played an important role in children's learning of positive customer values and their parents perceiving the influence as positive on their children's buying response. Both parents and children noted the impact of TV advertisements on children's purchase requests (Kapoor and Verma, 2004).

Teenage girls indicated that they exhibited competence in using environmental and knowledge-based resources "partially". This implies that if they revealed competency in some aspects of shopping, they came up short in other aspects they themselves perceived as being associated with shopping competence. The girls' responses also indicated that they were lacking in self-confidence and self-control, and this also moderated the degree to which the teenage girls utilized environmental and individual resources in achieving positive shopping outcomes (Mallalieu and Palan, 2006).

The young Indian is emerging as the biggest and most influential customer in the marketplace. Armed with an overload of information and entertainment options, they now induce parents, who grew up on a necessary consumption lifestyle to spend without a thought and challenge marketers to drum up stronger brand creation exercises. This is the age when channels like MTV belt out their favourite numbers at hours convenient to their segment, when multiplexes shy away from screening blockbusters during exam time, when customer giants like Unilever draw upon kid power to position a detergent as "dirt is good" and mobile operators play cupid with anonymous dates (Mukherji, 2006).

Children, especially tweens, are the largest customers of media and entertainment products. While adults spend just around two hours a day watching TV, kids are glued to the tube for over four hours a day. And, according to media analysis, they are much more involved viewers than adults, "Ad recall among kids is much higher than adults, simply because they are quite active viewers as against adults who are largely becoming passive T.V. customers" says Sandeep, Tarkas, CEO Media Direction (Srinivasan *et al.*, 2006, p. 54).

If India is a customer-based society today, where the adults are living it up, the juniors are not far behind: from pester power to direct consumption, the adolescent segment is driving consumption and forcing marketers to create new categories, product lines and service offerings. So from salons and gyms to exclusive clothes and jewellery lines, products are available for the very demanding market segment. The market for kids is evidently on a boil, if the numbers are to be believed (Bhupta and Pai, 2007). Adolescents are becoming as fashion conscious as their parents: it is no surprise that their preferences too are being addressed by top international brands. Proving the points are international brands like Reebok, Adidas, United Colors of Benetton and Kappa, which are offering kidswear based on animated characters, something that children can relate to (Sharma, 2008).

Adolescents influence the actual purchase decisions of food products. Child rearing practices differ from culture to culture and can be an important factor influencing the buying behaviour of families (Mahima and Khatri, 2008). More and more young couples are not only opting for nuclear families but are also happy having only one child. From something that was considered a rarity even 20 or 30 years ago, having a single child is fast becoming the norm in the urban milieu. This also makes sound financial sense in the current economic scenario wherein it is becoming imperative for both parents to be working so as to provide their child with the best of facilities; and the outcome of these changes is that an only child becomes the only centre of attention for the parents (Sachdeva, 2009).

The impact of TV advertising on pre-school and elementary school aged children occurs at multiple levels, including the relatively immediate product persuasion effects intended by the advertiser, as well as broader and/or more cumulative types of influences that accrue from exposure to a large number of commercials over time. For example, a cereal may have the immediate effect of generating product purchase requests and increasing product consumption, but it may also contribute to outcomes, such as misperceptions about proper nutritional habits. Celebrities and cartoon characters (zoo-zoo in the case of the advertisement for Vodafone) are commonly used by marketers, as children's views of advertising appeals are largely influenced by them. The practice is largely witnessed in restaurants giving a small toy as a token of remembrance to children such as McDonalds (Williams and Veeck, 1998) or associating a cartoon character with a cereal.

Only a few studies related to this topic, which have partially investigated the role of children along with other members in the household, is found in India. Verma (1982) partially investigated the role of family members for the purchase of a refrigerator. Singh (1992) studied the role played by family members while purchasing a TV. Singh (1998) further investigated the role of children as buyers and found that purchase requests by children are strongly stimulated by commercials or by a friend who has recently purchased a product. Kapoor (2001) investigated the influence of children in family purchase decisions for customer durables and, at the same time, Hundal (2001) examined the role of children while studying customer behaviour in the rural market. Singh and Kumar (2003) studied children as an emerging market in India and Kapoor and Verma (2005) investigated children's understanding of TV advertisements and the role of parent–child interaction on socialization of children. Mukherjee (2006) investigated family communication patterns, advertising attitudes and mediation behaviour with urban middle-class mothers.

3 Research Methodology

This chapter details the research methodology for the present study. It explains the overall design of the study, which includes the need for the study, its objectives, scope, phases of research and methodology adopted for carrying out the research work. The details of work done in each phase, tools, techniques and models used in the dissertation have also been presented in this chapter. The objectives of this study have been defined for studying the role of adolescents in family buying decision making.

3.1 Need for the Present Study

Based on the literature review, the need for the present study arises because the role of adolescents in a family's buying decision making has not been addressed. For this purpose, the present study is so designed to study and propose the adolescents' role in buying decision making and parents' perception towards their decisions.

The results of the study shall create an understanding on adolescents' buying behaviour. Merchandisers could get an idea about various factors influencing adolescents' behaviour towards consumption. Moreover, this study helps in comprehending the impact of various marketing activities on adolescents' behaviour: thus, enabling Indian academicians and government bodies to study and frame policies for protecting adolescents' duties and rights.

In addition to this, the role of computers and online marketing in adolescents' buying behaviour has been analysed as, in the present time, computers and the internet are the main consumer socialization agents.

3.2 Objectives of the Study

The following are the objectives of the study:

1   to study the role of consumer socialization agents for adolescents;

2   to study the relationship between adolescents' influence on family buying decision making and parent–adolescent communication patterns;
3   to examine the socio-economic factors that affect adolescents' buying decision making in Indian urban families;
4   to find out the influence tactics that adolescents employ in Indian urban families for fulfilling their demands;
5   to analyse the ways marketers use to influence adolescents' buying decision making.

3.3 Issues Explored in the Study

The following issues have been taken up during the research work:

1   defined consumer socialization agents with respect to demographic and socio-economic variables;
2   elaborated various consumer skills;
3   related the consumer socialization agents on consumer skills using suitable qualitative and quantitative techniques.

3.4 Scope of the Work

The scope of the work was limited to the urban families of Punjab, Haryana and the Union Territory of Chandigarh. The study is based on limited samples selected from different districts of Punjab, Haryana and Chandigarh. Districts were selected on the basis of population/literacy rate. States provided the first stage of the sampling unit, while the districts were the second stage, and parents and adolescents the third stage.

3.5 Methodology Adopted

For accomplishing the objectives of the study, the following methodology was adopted:

1   A detailed literature review was carried out to ascertain the significance of adolescents.
2   A survey of various families was carried out through a specially designed questionnaire for understanding and assessing the present situation.
3   Suitable qualitative and quantitative techniques were employed to analyse the prevailing situation.
4   The results were synthesized to come up with a suitable conclusion regarding adolescents' role in buying decision making and their parents' perception towards it.

Research is basically to determine new facts, through the process of dynamic changes in society. Methodology is described as a system of methods and rules to aid in collection and analysis of data. It provides a starting point for making a choice and approach made of concept, data, theories and definition of the topic (Hart, 1998).

Research Method

There are two basic research methods: qualitative research and quantitative research. Qualitative research is a process of enquiry with a goal of understanding a social or human problem. On the other hand, quantitative research is an enquiry about an identified problem, based on testing a theory to determine whether the productive generation of the theory holds true, using statistical techniques. In this study the qualitative research method involving the collection of a variety of empirical material, personal experiences, interviews and keen observation was used, based on adolescents and their parents being interviewed to learn about family buying decisions.

Research Design

As per, Claire Selltiz, research design should be such that it leads into logical conclusions. In this study both exploratory and descriptive research designs have been used. Descriptive studies involve the collection of data in order to answer the question regarding the current status of the subject of study.

The study involves large samples which have been used to give descriptions and define attitudes, opinions or behaviour that are measured and observed in a particular environment. The data has been collected in order to answer the questions regarding the current status of the subject of study.

The study also involves exploratory research design to give answer to the following questions "why and how". It is process of finding out what others feel and think about their words. It is concerned with gathering relevant facts and opinions. So, basically, the study involves exploratory research design which takes into consideration descriptive as well as exploratory data.

Sampling Design

Population is a key building block for a solid attributes sampling plan (Lindstrom, 2004). According to Lindstrom, auditors need to decide what to include in – and exclude from – the population, and the time period examined is an important consideration.

The purpose of this research is to examine how adolescents influence the family's purchase decisions. The sample of the study is based on the Multi Stage Stratified Random Sampling Technique. The adolescents and their parents are the ultimate stage of the sampling unit. Two questionnaires were framed: one for adolescents and one for any parent from the same family.

Size of the Sample

Sampling is described as the selection of a fraction of the total amount of units of interest to decision makers, for the ultimate purpose of being able to draw general conclusions about the entire body of units (Parasuraman, 1991).

The sample in the study is restricted to 800 respondents (one parent and one adolescent) from 400 units, keeping in mind the research objective and constraints.

Data Collection

Data is an important tool for the success of the study. In order to make meaningful research, a suitable methodology has to be adopted. Data collection is of two types, i.e. primary data and secondary data. The major part of the data is primary data in nature, collected through the use of questionnaires/scales. Secondary sources gather the information from various national/international journals, books, earlier related studies, reports and surveys of governments and non-government agencies: in this regard press releases, newspapers, periodicals and use of the internet explore various useful sites in relation to the study.

For the above said study, the data regarding various aspects of family purchase decisions was collected with the help of questionnaires prepared on the basis of like statements and opinions of experts on the related topics. These questionnaires/scales were used to collect the data through personal contact, i.e. survey method. The questionnaire was pre-tested to judge its reliability and validity.

The study is basically based on primary data; however sometimes secondary data was used wherever necessary. From the vast number of sampling units, we restricted the sample size to $400 \times 2 = 800$, keeping in mind the research objective, the plan of analysis, the constraint of time and resources at the disposal of the individual researcher.

Processing and Analysis of Data

The data was analysed by applying appropriate statistical techniques. The statistical tools include chi-square, Analysis of Variance (ANOVA), factor analysis (FA), *t*-test, etc. for analysing data to meet the objectives. Results and conclusions were drawn on the basis of analysis of data.

3.6 Phases of Research

Considering the complexity of the theme and taking into view the fact that such studies can be carried out primarily by closely following and analysing the approaches adopted by various organizations and results thereof, it was considered appropriate to carry out the study under the "Flexible Systems Methodology" (FSM) framework.

The three basic components of FSM are actor, situation and process (Sushil, 1994). The "situation" is to be managed by an "actor" through an appropriately evolved management "process", which recreates the situation. The "actor" forms a part of the "process" as well as the "situation". The research work involves the following phases.

Clarifying the Context

The detailed literature review has been conducted. The evolution of processes has been studied along with their relevance and shortcomings. The literature review illustrates tools, techniques employed in implementation processes of these factors and the potential benefits accrued by them.

Understanding and Assessing the Situation

A survey of a large number of adolescents and parents (400×2) has been completed through a specially prepared questionnaire for understanding and assessing the present situation. The survey design and analysis involves following steps:

1   Design of the questionnaire.
2   Pre-testing and validation of the questionnaire.
3   Data collection using the detailed "questionnaire" through postal mail, e-mail, personal visits, interviews and other communication means.
4   Summarizing and analysing the data to investigate the status of the role of adolescents in buying decision making.
5   Statistical analysis pertaining to the status of various performance indicators as a result of implementations. Suitable qualitative and quantitative techniques were employed to analyse the contributions of adolescents' in buying decision making.

Assessing the Actor's Capability

The survey was followed by qualitative and quantitative analysis in order to draw inferences for the role of adolescents in family buying decision making.

3.7 Framework

Figure 3.1 shows a block diagram for the methodology used for this research. This research was conducted in Punjab, Haryana and Chandigarh for studying the role of adolescents in family buying decision making. During this research, a large number of adolescents and their parents were surveyed for establishing inferences. The survey was conducted through a specially prepared questionnaire.

The approach was directed towards analysing the role of adolescents in family buying decision making. For completion of the survey effectively, the questionnaire was prepared through an extensive literature review and was validated through vast peer reviews from academicians. The questionnaire was based on five point Likert scale.

The questionnaires were forwarded to the organizations who were subsequently contacted through various communication means like: postal mail, e-mail, telephonic interviews, besides personal interviews through visits to various cities to facilitate responses to the questionnaire.

The responses were compiled and analysed to determine the role of adolescents in family buying decision making. In response to all these efforts, $400 \times 2 = 800$ filled questionnaires were received. A detailed description of the "questionnaire" is presented in the Appendix.

The various statistical tools, like response analysis, Cronbach's alpha, percent point score (PPS), ANOVA, t-test, chi-square, FA (including correlation) were employed for achieving the said objectives.

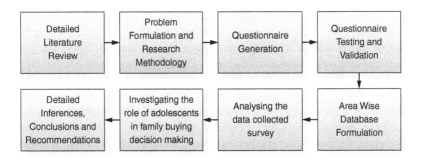

Figure 3.1 Block Diagram of Methodology.

The above work was extended by applying various qualitative techniques like Analytical Hierarchical Process (AHP), Technique for Order Preference by Similarity to Ideal Solution (TOPSIS) and *Vlse Kriterijumska Optimizacija I KOmpromisno Resenje* (VIKOR).

A summary of the research accomplishments has also been highlighted. Finally, limitations of the research have been presented and recommendations for future research directions have also been suggested.

3.8 Reliability and Validity

Reliability is defined as accuracy that a measure has in producing stable, consistent measurements. Since in social sciences scale is a reliable measurement, the social scientist must make sure that these scales are reliable measurements of the constructs they claim to measure.

3.8.1 Validity

Validity is the degree to which the instrument measures what it is intended to measure. As important as reliability is to measure, validity is even more important. There are three principal approaches to validity: face or content validity, predictive or concurrent validity and construct or factorial validity. In the study for development of a scale measuring parents' perception towards the role of adolescents in family purchase decisions, in the first instance efforts were made to improve and ensure the face validity of the scale by carrying out interviews and discussions with some experts in the target field (university researchers and professors in developmental psychology and education) and editing it again and again. Initially 50 items were chosen for the development scale measuring parents' perception towards the role of adolescents in family purchase decisions.

As in most of the prior studies, a five point Likert scale (1 = strongly disagree to 5 = strongly agree) was used as a response option from parents. All items underwent the judgment of experts who were given the definition of the proposed construct and were asked to identify: (1) any ambiguity in the wordings; (2) any incompatibility between an item and the dimension it was supposed to measure. Taking into account the comments and preferences received from experts, 29 items were selected. Construct validity was ensured by factorial validity. Factorial validity is based on the statistical technique known as "factor analysis". FA is a highly sophisticated statistical technique for examining a series of items to see which items correlate well with one another but are not highly correlated with other items or groups of items. McCroskey (2006) used this approach to measure attitudes towards communication sources. In the present study, construct validity was ensured through this technique for examining parents' perception of the influence of adolescents on the buying decisions in the family.

3.9 Pilot Study

After the selection of the data collection method, the particular methodology and scale to be used in the survey were formulated. In the initial phase of the study, several test surveys were carried out so as to list down various significant factors playing a central role in the study in hand. In these types of complex studies, it is better to examine various aspects with the help of pilot surveys. The initial scale includes various statements recorded during direct communication with the respondents, which later on helped to draft a final scale. The questionnaire was tested in two pilot studies.

It was decided to conduct a pilot study for the following reasons:

1   to identify the problem and revise the items to ensure that all questions were understandable to the respondents;
2   to test the method of measuring attitude (adolescents' influence in family buying decisions) which was later used in the main empirical research;
3   to finalize the scale to be used in the research;
4   to gain familiarity with the fieldwork and the problems that could occur at different stages of the research.

3.10 Statistical Framework

The data was analysed by applying both simple as well as advanced statistical techniques. The simple tools included frequencies, percentages and averages. Advanced statistical techniques included chi-square test, ANOVA, regression and FA. Results and conclusions were drawn on the basis of analysis of data.

3.10.1 Chi-Square Test

In order to see the association between two way distribution of respondents, the chi-square test was applied by using the following formula:

$$\chi^2 = \Sigma \frac{(O-E)^2}{E}$$

Where
χ^2 = chi-square value
O = observed frequency
E = expected frequency
Σ = summation

3.10.2 ANOVA

To compare more than two means at a time, ANOVA was carried out. This was done to compare a parameter between three regions, i.e. Punjab, Haryana and Chandigarh. The process of the analysis is given hereunder:

Source of Variation	df	TSS	MSS	F-ratio
Regions	$n-1=a$	S_1	$S1/a=x$	$x\|y$
Error	$b-a=c$	S_2	$S2/b=y$	
Total	$N-1=b$			

Where
n = number of regions to be compared, i.e. three
N = total number of respondents, i.e. 800
TSS = total sum of squares
MSS = mean sum of squares (TSS/df)
df = degree of freedom

3.10.3 Factor Analysis

FA is an interdependence technique in which all variables are simultaneously considered each related to others. Since the objective of this research was to summarize the variables, FA was applied. It studies the structure of interrelationships among a large number of variables by defining a set of common underlying latent dimensions known as factors. As a result, variables within each factor are more highly correlated with variables in that factor than with variables in other factors. This makes it possible to interpret the data from a much smaller number of factors than the original individual variables.

FA is a statistical method used to describe variability among observed variables in terms of a potentially lower number of unobserved variables called factors. In other words, it is possible, for example, that variations in three or four observed variables mainly reflect the variations in a single unobserved variable, or in a reduced number of unobserved variables. FA searches for such joint variations in response to unobserved latent variables. The observed variables are modelled as linear combinations of the potential factors, plus "error" terms. The information gained about the interdependencies between observed variables can be used later to reduce the set of variables in a dataset. FA originated in psychometrics, and is used in behavioural sciences, social sciences, marketing, product management, operations research and other applied sciences that deal with large quantities of data.

FA is related to principal component analysis (PCA), but the two are not identical. Because PCA performs a variance-maximizing rotation of the variable space, it takes into account all variability in the variables. In contrast, FA estimates how much of the variability is due to common factors ("communality"). The two methods become essentially equivalent if the error terms in the FA model (the variability not explained by common factors, see below) can be assumed to all have the same variance.

Mathematical Model

For $i=1, \ldots, 600$ the ith respondent's scores are

$$X1,i-\mu1*11\times600+L1,1Fi+L1,2F2+\varepsilon1,i$$
$$\vdots$$
$$Xn,i=\mu n*11\times600+ln,1Fi+ln,2F2+\varepsilon n,i$$

Where
xk,i is the ith respondent's score for the kth statement
μ_k is the mean of the respondents' scores for the kth statement
n is the number of statements
Fi is the ith respondent's "first factor"
$F2$ is the ith respondent's "second factor", and so on
$\varepsilon k,i$ is the difference between the ith respondent's score in the kth statement and the average score in the kth statement of all the respondents

In matrix notation, we have

$$X=\mu*11\times N+LF+\varepsilon$$

Where
N is number of respondents
X is a statement $\times$ number of respondents matrix of observable random variables
μ is a number of statements $\times 1$ column vector of unobservable constants
L is a statement $\times 2$ matrix of factor loadings
F is a $2\times$ consumers matrix of unobservable random variables
ε is a statement $\times$ respondents matrix of unobservable random variables

Type of Factoring

3.10.3.1 PCA

The most common form of FA, PCA seeks a linear combination of variables such that the maximum variance is extracted from the variables. It then removes this variance and seeks a second linear combination which explains the maximum proportion of the remaining variance, and so on. This is called the principal axis method and results in orthogonal (uncorrelated) factors.

3.10.3.2 Factor Loadings

The factor loadings, also called component loadings in PCA, are the correlation coefficients between the variables (rows) and factors (columns). Analogous to Pearson's *r*, the squared factor loading is the percentage of variance in that indicator variable explained by the factor. To get the percentage of variance in all the variables accounted for by each factor, add the sum of the squared factor loadings for that factor (column) and divide by the number of variables. (Note the number of variables equals the sum of their variances as the variance of a standardized variable is 1.) This is the same as dividing the factor's Eigen value by the number of variables.

3.10.3.3 Communality

The sum of the squared factor loadings for all factors for a given variable (row) is the variance in that variable accounted for by all the factors, and this is called the communality. The communality measures the percentage of variance in a given variable explained by all the factors jointly and may be interpreted as the reliability of the indicator.

3.10.3.4 Eigen Values

The Eigen value for a given factor measures the variance in all the variables which is accounted for by that factor. The ratio of Eigen values is the ratio of explanatory importance of the factors with respect to the variables. If a factor has a low Eigen value, then it is contributing little to the explanation of variances in the variables and may be ignored as redundant with more important factors. Eigen values measure the amount of variation in the total sample accounted for by each factor.

3.10.3.5 Factor Scores

Factor scores (also called component scores in PCA) are the scores of each case (row) on each factor (column). To compute the factor score for a given case for a given factor, one takes the case's standardized score on each variable, multiplies by the corresponding factor loading of the variable for the given factor, and sums these products. Computing factor scores allows one to look for factor outliers. Also, factor scores may be used as variables in subsequent modelling.

3.10.3.6 Criteria for Determining the Number of Factors

Varimax rotation is an orthogonal rotation of the factor axes to maximize the variance of the squared loadings of a factor (column) on all the variables (rows) in a factor matrix, which has the effect of differentiating the original variables by extracted factor. Each factor tends to have either large or small loadings of any particular variable. A varimax solution yields results which make it as easy as possible to identify each variable with a single factor. This is the most common rotation option.

3.10.3.7 Reliable Measurements

The variables should first be measured on interval level. Second, the variables should be normally distributed; which makes it possible to "generalize the results of analysis beyond the sample collected". Third, the sample size should be taken into consideration, as correlations are not resistant (Moore and McCabe, 2006) and can hence seriously influence the reliability of the FA. The most important factors in determining reliable factor solutions were the absolute sample size and the absolute magnitude of factor loadings. Field (2000) states that a researcher should have at least 10–15 subjects per variable. Habing (2003) stated that a researcher should have at least 50 observations and at least five times as many observations as variables. In the study these considerations were duly taken into account. The scales were framed keeping the above considerations.

3.11 Scoring of the Variables

Before going for data analysis, different variables were developed by assigning scores to the attributes. This was done as shown in Table 3.1.

Table 3.1 Scales Used for Variables

Scales Used	Score
Strongly Agree	5
Agree	4
Indifferent	3
Disagree	2
Strongly Disagree	1

Note: Interval scale used to assess media exposure among adolescents

4 Data Analysis and Interpretation

In this chapter *data analysis and results interpretation* for adolescents' role in family buying decision making is presented. This chapter describes the analysis performed to attain the desired objectives of the study. Statistical Package for Social Sciences (SPSS) 21.0 (now called PASW (Predictive Analytics Software)) is the statistical tool used for applying different statistical techniques. Various statistical techniques applied are: *t*-test, ANOVA, chi-square, PPS, central tendency, FA, correlation, AHP, TOPSIS and VIKOR. The internal consistency, that is, how closely a set of variables are related in a group, of the questionnaire is measured by employing Cronbach alpha.

4.1 Cronbach Alpha

Cronbach alpha is used to estimate the proportion of variance. The higher the coefficient, the more is reliability of the generated questionnaire. Nunnaly (1978) has specified 0.7 as an acceptable reliability coefficient but, sometimes, lower coefficients are also used. Reliability index is evaluated for different sections of the questionnaire which are: adolescents, parents and for the overall questionnaire. It can range from 0.00 (if no variance is consistent) to 1.00 (if all variance is consistent) For example, if the Cronbach alpha for a set of scores turns out to be 0.90, it means that the test is 90% reliable, and by extension that it is 10% unreliable. The value of alpha greater than or equal to 0.9 means internal consistency is excellent, between 0.7 and 0.9 means good, between 0.6 and 0.7 means acceptable, between 0.5 and 0.6 means poor, and less than 0.5 is unacceptable.

According to the response from the respondents, the value of Cronbach alpha came to be 0.975 for the overall questionnaire, as shown in Table 4.1, which means internal consistency between the factors is excellent.

Table 4.1 Cronbach Alpha Reliability Index of Questionnaire

Part A: Adolescents	0.955
Part B: Parents	0.943
Overall	0.975

4.2 Demographic Profile

Before the perceptions of adolescents and their parents are elaborated, it is quite relevant to have an overview of the demographic profile as it may have an impact on the perceptions about adolescents' role in family buying decision making. The distribution of respondents according to various demographic variables is as follows.

4.2.1 Gender

Figure 4.1 shows state-wise data of gender for various respondents.

Table 4.2(a) shows the gender of the respondents. A total of 58% of the total respondents were males and 42% were females. A similar pattern was also depicted when comparing state-wise data: there were 57.3% males from Punjab, 53% males from Chandigarh and 62% males from Haryana. The mean male respondents were 77.33 and females were 56.

Further Table 4.2(b) shows ANOVA results. Similar results have been given by ANOVA (f-test) as the f-value comes out to be 1.01792 and the corresponding p-value of 0.459. There is always a probabilistic component involved in the accept–reject decision in testing a hypothesis.

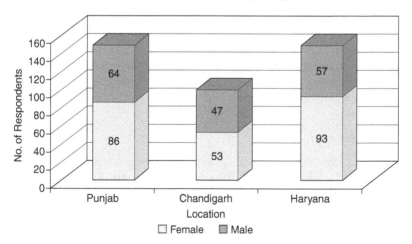

Figure 4.1 State-Wise Comparison of Gender Data.

Table 4.2(a) Gender Data

	Male	Female
Punjab	86	64
Chandigarh	53	47
Haryana	93	57
Mean	77.33	56
t-value	1.60603	
Chi-square	2.0389	

Table 4.2(b) ANOVA for Gender Data

Result Details

Source	SS	df	MS	
Between treatments	833.3333	2	416.6667	$F = 1.01792$
Within treatments	1228	3	409.3333	
Total	2,061.3333	5		

The criterion that is used for accepting or rejecting a null hypothesis is called significance level or *p*-value. The *p*-value represents the probability of concluding (incorrectly) that there is a difference in your samples when no true difference exists. In other words, a *p*-value of 0.05 means there is only a 5% chance that you would be wrong in concluding that the populations are different or 95% confident of making a right decision.

It is concluded that the mean data was statistically at par as indicated by the *t*-value of 1.60 and even a chi-square value of 2.03 also indicated the same. Also, the data being not significant at $p < 0.05$ that is, there is not much difference in the views of different respondents belonging to different regions and gender.

4.2.2 Education

Figure 4.2 shows state-wise data of education for various respondents.

Table 4.3(a) shows the education of the respondents. A total of 38.75% of the total respondents were from schools and 61.25% were from college. A similar pattern was also depicted when comparing state-wise data: 43.3%, 37% and 35.3% were from schools of Punjab, Chandigarh and Haryana respectively. The mean respondents from schools were 51.67 and colleges were 81.67.

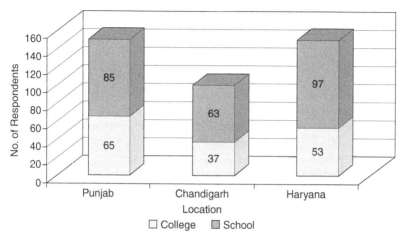

Figure 4.2 State-Wise Data of Education Levels.

Table 4.3(a) Education Data

	School	College
Punjab	65	85
Chandigarh	37	63
Haryana	53	97
Mean	51.67	81.67
t-value	1.83628	
Chi-square	1.1944	

Table 4.3(b) ANOVA for Education Data

Result Details

Source	SS	df	MS	
Between treatments	833.3333	2	416.6667	F=0.83001
Within treatments	1506	3	502	
Total	2,339.3333	5		

Further Table 4.3(b) shows ANOVA results. Similar results have been given by ANOVA (*f*-test) as the *f*-value comes out to be 0.83001 and the corresponding *p*-value of 0.516534.

In nutshell, the mean data was statistically at par as indicated by the *t*-value of 1.83 and even chi-square value of 1.19 also indicated the same.

Also, the data being not significant at $p<0.05$ that is, there is not much difference in the views of different respondents belonging to different regions and education level.

4.2.3 Age

Table 4.4(a) shows the age of the respondents. The average age of the total respondents is 14.99. A similar pattern was also depicted when comparing state-wise data: the average age for Punjab, Chandigarh and Haryana was 14.64, 15.15 and 15.24 respectively.

Further Table 4.4(b) shows ANOVA results. Similar results have been given by ANOVA (*f*-test) as the *f*-value comes out to be 1.771 and the corresponding *p*-value of 0.63778.

It is concluded that the mean age of the three regions is almost similar and the data being not significant at $p<0.05$ that is, there is not much difference in the views of different respondents belonging to different regions and age.

Table 4.4(a) Age Data

Age	Punjab (Freq.)	Chandigarh (Freq.)	Haryana (Freq.)	Total (Freq.)
10	5	4	4	13
11	7	6	9	22
12	18	7	10	35
13	14	9	13	36
14	21	11	17	49
15	33	15	25	73
16	22	15	21	58
17	15	13	22	50
18	10	12	16	38
19	5	8	13	26
Mean age	14.64	15.15	15.24	14.99

Table 4.4(b) ANOVA for Age Data

Result Details

Source	SS	df	MS	
Between treatments	30.3075	2	15.1538	$F=1.77151$
Within treatments	2,170.67	397	5.4677	
Total	2,200.9775	399		

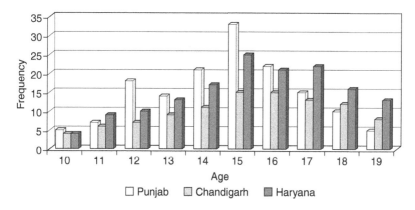

Figure 4.3 State-Wise Comparison of Age.

Figure 4.3 shows state-wise comparison of age of respondents.

4.2.4 Father's Qualification

Figure 4.4 shows state-wise data of father's qualification for various respondents.

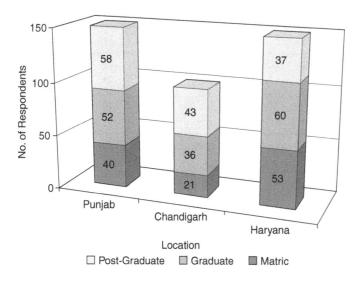

Figure 4.4 State-Wise Comparison of Father's Qualification Data.

Table 4.5(a) shows the father's qualification of the respondents. A total of 28.5% of the total respondents were matric pass, 36.9% were graduate and 34.5% were post-graduate. A similar pattern was also depicted when comparing state-wise data: there were 26.66%, 21% and 35% matric pass Punjab, Chandigarh and Haryana respectively. The mean male respondents were 38 matric pass, 49.33 graduate and 46 post-graduate.

Further Table 4.5(b) shows ANOVA results. Similar results have been given by ANOVA (*f*-test) as the *f*-value comes out to be 1.3855 and the corresponding *p*-value of 0.172857.

It is concluded that the mean data was statistically at par as indicated by a chi-square value of 1.2739. Also, the data being not significant at $p < 0.05$ that is, there is not much difference in the views of different respondents belonging to different regions and father's qualification.

4.2.5 Father's Occupation

Table 4.6(a) shows the father's occupation of the respondents. A total of 39% of the total respondents were businessmen, 48% were in service and 13% responded "N.A." A similar pattern was also depicted when comparing state-wise data: there were 37.33%, 50.66% and 12% businessmen, in service and N.A. respectively in respondents from Punjab. The mean businessmen respondents were 52 and 64 in service.

Table 4.5(a) Father's Qualification Data

	Matric	Graduate	Post-Graduate
Punjab	40	52	58
Chandigarh	21	36	43
Haryana	53	60	37
Mean	38	49.33	46
Chi-square	1.2739		

Table 4.5(b) ANOVA for Father's Qualification Data

Result Details				
Source	SS	df	MS	
Between treatments	555.5556	2	277.7778	F = 1.3855
Within treatments	698.6667	6	116.4444	
Total	1254.2222	8		

Further Table 4.6(b) shows ANOVA results. Similar results have been given by ANOVA (*f*-test) as the *f*-value comes out to be 0.45257 and the corresponding *p*-value of 0.656049.

Figure 4.5 shows state-wise data of Father's Occupation for various respondents.

Table 4.6(a) Father's Occupation Data

	Business	*Service*	*N.A.*
Punjab	56	76	18
Chandigarh	39	48	13
Haryana	61	68	21
Mean	52	64	17.33
Chi-square	0.8889		

Table 4.6(b) ANOVA for Father's Occupation Data

Result Details

Source	*SS*	*df*	*MS*	
Between treatments	555.5556	2	277.7778	*F* = 0.45257
Within treatments	3682.6667	6	613.7778	
Total	4238.2222	8		

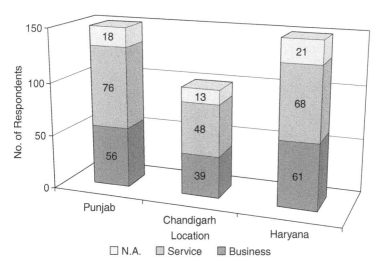

Figure 4.5 State-Wise Comparison of Father's Occupation Data.

It is concluded that the mean data was statistically at par as indicated by a chi-square value of 0.8889. Also, the data being not significant at $p < 0.05$ that is, there is not much difference in the views of different respondents belonging to different regions and father's occupation.

4.2.6 Mother's Qualification

Figure 4.6 shows state-wise data of mother's qualification for various respondents.

Table 4.7(a) shows the mother's qualification of the respondents. A total of 19.98% of the total respondents were matric pass, 44.74% were graduate and 36.24% were post-graduate. A similar pattern was also depicted when compared state-wise data: there were 12.66%, 46% and 41.33% matric pass, graduate and post-graduate from Punjab respectively. The mean male respondents were 25.33 matric pass, 59.66 graduate and 48.33 post-graduate.

Further Table 4.7(b) shows ANOVA results. Similar results have been given by ANOVA (*f*-test) as the *f*-value comes out to be 0.65963 and the corresponding *p*-value of 0.550874.

It is concluded that the mean data was statistically at par as indicated by a chi-square value of 1.8761. Also, the data being not significant at $p < 0.05$ that is, there is not much difference in the views of different respondents belonging to different regions and mother's qualification.

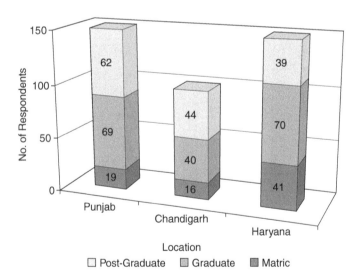

Figure 4.6 State-Wise Comparison of Mother's Qualification Data.

Table 4.7(a) Mother's Qualification Data

	Matric	*Graduate*	*Post-Graduate*
Punjab	19	69	62
Chandigarh	16	40	44
Haryana	41	70	39
Mean	25.33	59.66	48.33
Chi-square	1.8761		

Table 4.7(b) ANOVA for Mother's Qualification Data

Result Details

Source	SS	df	MS	
Between treatments	555.5556	2	277.7778	$F = 0.65963$
Within treatments	2526.6667	6	421.1111	
Total	3082.2222	8		

4.2.7 Mother's Occupation

Table 4.8(a) shows the mother's occupation of the respondents. A total of 54% of the total respondents were in service and 46% were housewives. A similar pattern was also depicted when compared state-wise data: there were 54.49% and 45.49% in service and housewives respectively in respondents from Punjab. The mean service women respondents were 72.66 and 60.66 were housewives.

Figure 4.7 shows state-wise data of mother's occupation for various respondents.

Further Table 4.8(b) shows ANOVA results. Similar results have been given by ANOVA (*f*-test) as the *f*-value comes out to be 1.46429 and the corresponding *p*-value of 0.126124.

Table 4.8(a) Mother's Occupation Data

	Service	*Housewife*
Punjab	81	69
Chandigarh	60	40
Haryana	77	73
Mean	72.66	60.66
t-value	0.98125	
Chi-square	1.8416	

88   *Data Analysis and Interpretation*

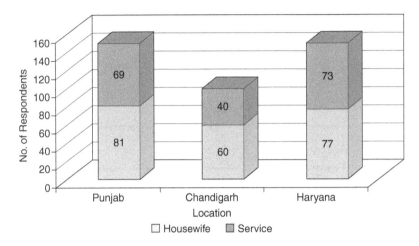

Figure 4.7 State-Wise Comparison of Mother's Occupation Data.

Table 4.8(b) ANOVA for Mother's Occupation Data

Result Details

Source	SS	df	MS	
Between treatments	833.3333	2	416.6667	$F = 1.46429$
Within treatments	280	3	93.3333	
Total	1113.3333	5		

It has been concluded that the mean data was statistically at par as indicated by *t*-value of 0.98 and even chi-square value of 1.84 that also indicated the same. Also, the data being not significant at $p < 0.05$ that is, there is not much difference in the views of different respondents belonging to different regions and occupation.

4.2.8 Annual Income

Figure 4.8 shows state-wise data of annual income for various respondents.

Table 4.9(a) shows the annual income of the respondents. A total of 16.24% of the total respondents had income up to 2 Lakhs, 28.50% had income of 2–5 Lakhs, 38.75% had income of 5–10 Lakhs and 18.67% had income above 10 lakhs. A similar pattern was also depicted when comparing

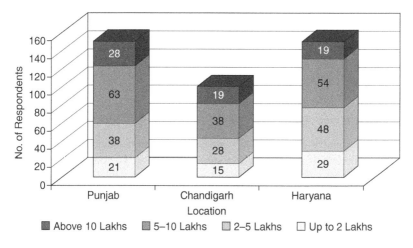

Figure 4.8 State-Wise Comparison of Annual Income Data.

Table 4.9(a) Annual Income Data

Location	Up to 2 Lakhs	2–5 Lakhs	5–10 Lakhs	Above 10 Lakhs
Punjab	21	38	63	28
Chandigarh	15	28	38	19
Haryana	29	48	54	19
Mean	21.66	38	51.66	22
Chi-square	1.4799			

Table 4.9(b) ANOVA for Annual Income Data

Result Details

Source	SS	df	MS	
Between treatments	416.6667	2	208.3333	$F = 0.88277$
Within treatments	2,124	9	236	
Total	2,540.6667	11		

state-wise data: 14%, 25.33%, 42% and 18.67% had income up to 2 Lakhs, 2–5 Lakhs, 5–10 Lakhs and above 10 Lakhs respectively in respondents from Punjab. The mean of respondents having income up to 2 Lakhs were 21.66, 2–5 Lakhs were 38, 5–10 Lakhs were 51.66 and above 10 Lakhs were 22. Further, Table 4.9(b) shows ANOVA results. Similar results have been given by ANOVA (f-test) as the f-value comes out to be 0.88277 and the corresponding p-value of 0.446612.

In a nutshell, the mean data was statistically at par as indicated by a chi-square value of 1.4799. Also, the data being not significant at $p<0.05$ that is, there is not much difference in the views of different respondents belonging to different regions and annual income.

4.3 Response Analysis

The surveyed respondents were assessed on various statements based on the parameters of the adolescents' decision making. The data was collected from the respondents on five-point scale, i.e. strongly disagree (1), disagree (2), indifferent (3), agree (4), strongly agree (5).

It has been observed that the average PPS of the whole questionnaire is 55.468 and average central tendency of the whole questionnaire is 2.77 as shown in Table 4.10.

4.4 Factor Analysis

FA and PCA techniques are used when the researcher is interested in identifying a smaller number of factors underlying a large number of observed variables. Variables that have a high correlation between them and are largely independent of other subsets of variables, are combined into factors. A common usage of PCA and FA is in developing objective instruments for measuring constructs which are not directly observable in real life.

Factor and Component

Factors are produced by FA, while components are produced by PCA. Both FA and PCA essentially are data reduction techniques. Mathematically, the difference is in the variance of the observed variables that is analysed. In PCA, all the variance in the observed variables is analysed whereas in FA, only shared variance is analysed. Even though PCA is different from other techniques of FA, at many places it is treated as one of the FA techniques.

Exploratory and Confirmatory Factor Analysis

As the name suggests, in exploratory FA (EFA) we are interested in exploring the underlying dimensions that could have caused correlations among the observed variables. In case of confirmatory FA (CFA), the researcher is interested in testing whether the correlations among the observed variables are consistent with the hypothesized factor structure.

Thus, while EFA deals with theory building, CFA deals with theory testing.

Factor Extraction

Extraction refers to the process of obtaining underlying factors or components. Besides PCA, SPSS offers several other extraction methods such as principal axis factoring (PAF), alpha factoring etc. The differences are primarily mathematical in nature and generate similar results in most of the cases. The two most commonly used extraction methods are PCA and PAF. If the researcher has designed the study based on a theoretical consideration, PFA should be the preferred choice. However, if the main aim of the researcher is simply to reduce the number of variables, PCA is a better choice.

The Eigen values associated with each component represents variance explained by that particular linear component and displays the Eigen value in terms of the percentage of variance. It is clear that the large amount of variance is explained by the first few components whereas the rest of the components explain only a small amount of variance.

Only five components are extracted as shown. In Tables 4.14(a) and 4.22(a), extractions sum of squared loadings, the values are the same as the values before extraction, except values for the discarded components are ignored. In the last column rotation sums of squared loadings, the Eigen values of the components after rotation are displayed.

Communality gives the variance accounted for a particular variable by all the factors. Mathematically, it is the sum of squared loadings for a variable across all the factors. The higher the value of communality for a particular variable after extraction, the higher is its amount of variance explained by the extracted factors.

Factor Loadings

FA produces factor loadings for each combination of extracted factors and the observed variables. Factor loadings are similar to correlation coefficients between the factors and the variables. Thus, the higher the factor loading, the more likely it is that the factor underlies that variable. Factor loadings help in identifying which variables are associated with the particular factors.

Rotation

Factor loadings obtained from extraction may not present a clear picture of the factor structure of the dataset. After extraction, while we may be able to identify the number of factors, we may not know the exact way in which

Table 4.10 Percent Point Score

PART A: ADOLESCENTS

No.	Factors	No. of Respondents Scoring Points					Total No. of Responses (N)	Total Points Scored (TPS)**	Percent Points Score (PPS) $\frac{TPS}{5*N}$ 100	Central Tendency TPS/N
		A 1	B 2	C 3	D 4	E 5				
1	Father has a right to accept or reject any purchase decision at any time	16	128	136	88	32	400	1192	59.6	2.98
2	Parents can easily impose their decision on their adolescents	48	160	128	24	40	400	1048	52.4	2.62
3	Family member has his/her ideas relating to the products to be purchased	64	112	160	32	32	400	1056	52.8	2.64
4	Parents feel that you are the younger generation and hence more aware to take your own decisions	72	136	96	48	48	400	1064	53.2	2.66
5	Parents generally allow you to buy daily need products of your choice	56	168	64	56	56	400	1088	54.4	2.72
6	Parents appreciate the things purchased by you	40	176	80	56	48	400	1096	54.8	2.74
7	Parents feel dissatisfied regarding modified use of products after buying it	80	64	112	112	32	400	1152	57.6	2.88
8	Since you are an important member of the family, you have the right to initiate and influence and also to decide sometimes regarding the purchase decision	32	184	72	48	64	400	1128	56.4	2.82
9	Family members are egoistic about their self-concept in purchase matters	72	176	72	32	48	400	1008	50.4	2.52
10	Educated members play an effective role in the decision making process	80	112	144	32	32	400	1024	51.2	2.56
11	Change in income causes change in the buying behaviour	64	168	96	32	40	400	1016	50.8	2.54
12	Major part of the family income is spent by the adolescents	24	144	160	40	32	400	1112	55.6	2.78
13	You give your consent in buying the costly products in the family	96	72	96	64	72	400	1144	57.2	2.86

#	Statement									
14	Are you the initiator/problem recognizer and hence the first person to demand the product	40	144	88	96	32	400	1136	56.8	2.84
15	Switch from one brand to another for adventure	88	144	80	48	40	400	1008	50.4	2.52
16	Advertisements have comparatively more impact on the minds of adolescents	16	200	72	64	48	400	1128	56.4	2.82
17	Promotional schemes like advertisements always lure you to buy the products	64	144	112	48	32	400	1040	52	2.6
18	Rapid growth of market for adolescents' products is important	32	88	160	32	88	400	1256	62.8	3.14

The following source of information influences purchasing Personal Consumable Items like Gum, Candies, Chocolates, Ice Cream, Cold Drinks

19	TV advertisements	72	120	104	24	80	400	1120	56	2.8
20	Friends	16	128	144	64	48	400	1200	60	3
21	Internet	104	136	72	32	56	400	1000	50	2.5
22	Visit to Store	56	96	112	104	32	400	1160	58	2.9
23	Parents	104	88	96	48	64	400	1080	54	2.7

The following source of information influences purchasing Personal Durable Items like Shoes, Clothes, Video Games, School Stationery, Computer Games

24	TV advertisements	80	144	96	48	32	400	1008	50.4	2.52
25	Friends	56	152	128	40	24	400	1024	51.2	2.56
26	Internet	40	160	136	32	32	400	1056	52.8	2.64
27	Visit to store	56	128	112	64	40	400	1104	55.2	2.76
28	Parents	24	112	152	48	64	400	1216	60.8	3.04

The following source of information influences purchasing Family Toiletries Items like Toothpaste, Soap, Shampoo, Cosmetics, Deodorant, Laundry Soap

29	TV advertisements	96	136	64	40	64	400	1040	52	2.6
30	Friends	40	160	128	40	32	400	1064	53.2	2.66
31	Internet	48	80	120	88	64	400	1240	62	3.1
32	Visit to store	48	88	136	80	48	400	1192	59.6	2.98
33	Parents	72	160	48	56	64	400	1080	54	2.7

The following source of information influences purchasing Family Electronics Items like TV, Refrigerator, Telephone, Computer, DVD

34	TV advertisements	24	64	160	96	56	400	1296	64.8	3.24
35	Friends	88	152	56	64	40	400	1016	50.8	2.54
36	Internet	96	112	120	40	32	400	1000	50	2.5

continued

Table 4.10 Continued

No.	Factors	No. of Respondents Scoring Points					Total No. of Responses (N)	Total Points Scored (TPS)**	Percent Points Score (PPS) $\frac{TPS}{5*N}$ 100	Central Tendency TPS/N
		A	B	C	D	E				
		1	2	3	4	5				
The following source of information influences purchasing Family Automobile Items like Car, Scooter, Motorcycle, Bicycle										
39	TV advertisements	104	64	72	80	80	400	1168	58.4	2.92
40	Friends	32	104	192	48	24	400	1128	56.4	2.82
41	Internet	24	144	160	16	56	400	1136	56.8	2.84
42	Visit to store	40	144	128	64	24	400	1088	54.4	2.72
43	Parents	24	104	152	104	16	400	1184	59.2	2.96
The following source of information influences purchasing Other Product or Activities like Movie Visit, Restaurant, Vacation										
44	TV advertisements	48	152	88	80	32	400	1096	54.8	2.74
45	Friends	16	128	144	88	24	400	1176	58.8	2.94
46	Internet	8	112	160	80	40	400	1232	61.6	3.08
47	Visit to store	112	80	128	48	32	400	1008	50.4	2.52
48	Parents	96	104	64	72	64	400	1104	55.2	2.76
You influence decisions when buying personal consumable items										
49	Gum, candies, chocolates	88	128	96	48	40	400	1024	51.2	2.56
50	Ice creams	80	112	104	32	72	400	1104	55.2	2.76
51	Soft drinks/cold Drink	24	112	152	72	40	400	1192	59.6	2.98
52	Health drinks	24	144	120	80	32	400	1152	57.6	2.88
53	Fast foods (noodles, pasta)	80	144	72	72	32	400	1032	51.6	2.58
You have an influence when buying durable items										
54	Shoes and footwear	40	88	160	80	32	400	1176	58.8	2.94
55	Adolescents' clothes	112	112	80	56	40	400	1000	50	2.5
56	School bags	96	128	88	56	32	400	1000	50	2.5
57	Toys and video games (PC2/PC3)	40	136	144	48	32	400	1096	54.8	2.74
58	Stationery items like pencils, pens	96	136	80	48	40	400	1000	50	2.5
59	Magazine and comics	24	112	104	80	80	400	1280	64	3.2

You influence buying following products

60	Go to movie	16	80	168	72	64	400	1288	64.4	3.22
61	Restaurant	24	112	144	72	48	400	1208	60.4	3.02
62	Family vacations	24	168	96	56	56	400	1152	57.6	2.88
63	Visiting to malls and supermarkets	56	136	128	48	32	400	1064	53.2	2.66

Following source is important for *Entertainment*

64	Magazine	16	96	232	48	8	400	1136	56.8	2.84
65	Newspaper	88	104	80	72	56	400	1104	55.2	2.76
66	Internet	96	152	48	40	64	400	1024	51.2	2.56
67	TV	88	112	128	56	16	400	1000	50	2.5
68	Radio	48	144	104	48	56	400	1120	56	2.8

Following source is important for *Homework*

69	Magazine	72	136	120	40	32	400	1024	51.2	2.56
70	Newspaper	96	96	128	64	16	400	1008	50.4	2.52
71	Internet	8	104	128	112	48	400	1288	64.4	3.22
72	TV	16	96	144	112	32	400	1248	62.4	3.12
73	Radio	56	144	72	72	56	400	1128	56.4	2.82

Following source is important for *Sports related information*

74	Magazine	16	48	192	128	16	400	1280	64	3.2
75	Newspaper	24	88	120	128	40	400	1272	63.6	3.18
76	Internet	24	136	112	104	24	400	1168	58.4	2.92
77	TV	72	120	160	24	24	400	1008	50.4	2.52
78	Radio	48	80	208	24	40	400	1128	56.4	2.82

Following source is important for *Cartoon*

79	Magazine	16	192	80	80	32	400	1120	56	2.8
80	Newspaper	48	168	64	80	40	400	1096	54.8	2.74
81	Internet	24	184	144	16	32	400	1048	52.4	2.62
82	TV	24	176	120	48	32	400	1088	54.4	2.72
83	Radio	16	128	136	88	32	400	1192	59.6	2.98

continued

Table 4.10 Continued

No.	Factors	No. of Respondents Scoring Points					Total No. of Responses (N)	Total Points Scored (TPS)**	Percent Points Score (PPS) $\frac{TPS}{5*N}$ 100	Central Tendency TPS/N
		A	B	C	D	E				
		1	2	3	4	5				
You give importance to different kinds of appeals and demonstrations present in TV advertisements										
84	Emotional appeal depicting social status like presence of celebrity in the advertisements	48	160	128	24	40	400	1048	52.4	2.62
85	Emotional appeal depicting catchy phrases and words in the form of jingles and slogans	64	112	160	32	32	400	1056	52.8	2.64
86	Emotional appeal depicting use of adventure/action and thrilling scenes	72	136	96	48	48	400	1064	53.2	2.66
87	Emotional appeal depicting presence of striking scenes of nature scenes (mountains, flowing streams, etc.)	56	168	64	56	56	400	1088	54.4	2.72
You behave in the following manner to get the advertised product from your parents										
88	I make a very polite request to them	40	176	80	56	48	400	1096	54.8	2.74
89	I keep on asking or saying please, please unless I get it	80	64	112	112	32	400	1152	57.6	2.88
90	I make a direct request without explaining them any reason	32	184	72	48	64	400	1128	56.4	2.82
91	I make money deals or labour deals in exchange for my purchases	72	176	72	32	48	400	1008	50.4	2.52
92	I say that everyone has it like all my friends use it	80	112	144	32	32	400	1024	51.2	2.56
93	I do good deeds like cleaning the room	64	168	96	32	40	400	1016	50.8	2.54
94	Acting affectionate like hugging them or saying how nice they look or showing too much love	24	144	160	40	32	400	1112	55.6	2.78
95	I get mad and slam door or display anger verbally or non-verbally	96	72	96	64	72	400	1144	57.2	2.86
96	I try to influence them through some people like aunts, grandparents who can convince them	40	144	88	96	32	400	1136	56.8	2.84
97	I act sad and go to my room and cry	88	144	80	48	40	400	1008	50.4	2.52

Please tick whether you agree or disagree to the following statements

98	TV advertisements are a valuable source of information to me	16	200	72	64	48	400	1128	56.4	2.82
99	I find TV advertisements quite amusing and entertaining	64	144	112	48	32	400	1040	52	2.6
100	Sometimes I find TV advertisements are more enjoyable as compared to other media content	32	88	160	32	88	400	1256	62.8	3.14
101	I would like to buy the brands advertised on TV	72	120	104	24	80	400	1120	56	2.8
102	TV advertisements inform me about latest fashion trends	16	128	144	64	48	400	1200	60	3
103	I like catchy punch lines in TV advertisements	104	136	72	32	56	400	1000	50	2.5
104	I often ask my parents to buy what I saw in commercials	56	96	112	104	32	400	1160	58	2.9
105	TV advertisements persuade me to like the product	104	88	96	48	64	400	1080	54	2.7

PART B: PARENTS

106	Adolescents want liberty of expression	80	144	96	48	32	400	1008	50.4	2.52
107	Advertisement and media influence buying decision making	56	152	128	40	24	400	1024	51.2	2.56
108	Purchase decision in a family is taken as one entity	40	160	136	32	32	400	1056	52.8	2.64
109	You agree to the consent of your adolescents, while buying a household product	56	128	112	64	40	400	1104	55.2	2.76
110	In your family most of routine decisions are initiated by adolescents	24	112	152	48	64	400	1216	60.8	3.04
111	Mother and adolescents are able to finance some of the purchase decisions rejected by the father	96	136	64	40	64	400	1040	52	2.6
112	Adolescents oblige the financial conditions of the family	40	160	128	40	32	400	1064	53.2	2.66
113	The actual buyers of the product are as much aware as the adolescents	48	80	120	88	64	400	1240	62	3.1
114	Adolescents do not care for their needs and desires	48	88	136	80	48	400	1192	59.6	2.98
115	Increasing use of TV, cinema affects the decision making role of the adolescents	72	160	48	56	64	400	1080	54	2.7
116	When the personal consumption is individual, the other family members take part in the decision	24	64	160	96	56	400	1296	64.8	3.24
117	Adolescents have quick buying decisions	88	152	56	64	40	400	1016	50.8	2.54

continued

Table 4.10 Continued

No.	Factors	No. of Respondents Scoring Points					Total No. of Responses (N)	Total Points Scored (TPS)**	Percent Points Score (PPS) $\frac{TPS}{5*N}$ 100	Central Tendency TPS/N
		A	B	C	D	E				
		1	2	3	4	5				
118	Adolescents are highly brand conscious	96	112	120	40	32	400	1000	50	2.5
119	Adolescents are highly affected by physical attributes of a product	80	152	72	64	32	400	1016	50.8	2.54
120	The cultural shift has brought about a change in the decision making process	64	128	104	64	40	400	1088	54.4	2.72
121	The household income plays role in the decision making process for a purchase made for the adolescents	104	64	72	80	80	400	1168	58.4	2.92
122	Adolescents are early adopters and make decisions in hurry	32	104	192	48	24	400	1128	56.4	2.82
123	Adolescents play the role of mediator in any type of conflict in the decisions of the parents	24	144	160	16	56	400	1136	56.8	2.84
124	You rely upon the information provided by your adolescents as you feel they are more updated because of media	40	144	128	64	24	400	1088	54.4	2.72
125	Adolescents help in providing a final effect to the purchase decisions	24	104	152	104	16	400	1184	59.2	2.96
126	Adolescents try to acquire appropriate knowledge about the product before they create an influence for change	48	152	88	80	32	400	1096	54.8	2.74
127	Role models are important in adolescents' buying decisions	16	128	144	88	24	400	1176	58.8	2.94
	The following activities influence adolescents' buying behaviour									
128	Watching TV	8	112	160	80	40	400	1232	61.6	3.08
129	Using internet	112	80	128	48	32	400	1008	50.4	2.52
130	Reading newspaper/magazines	96	104	64	72	64	400	1104	55.2	2.76
131	Listening to the radio/FM	88	128	96	48	40	400	1024	51.2	2.56
132	Online shopping	80	112	104	32	72	400	1104	55.2	2.76

While making a buying decision you pay attention towards following advertising media

133	TV commercials	24	112	152	72	40	400	1192	59.6	2.98
134	Newspaper advertisement	24	144	120	80	32	400	1152	57.6	2.88
135	Advertisements on vehicles	80	144	72	72	32	400	1032	51.6	2.58
136	Magazine advertisement	40	88	160	80	32	400	1176	58.8	2.94
137	Billboard advertisement	112	112	80	56	40	400	1000	50	2.5
138	Radio advertisement	96	128	88	56	32	400	1000	50	2.5
139	Browser advertisement	40	136	144	48	32	400	1096	54.8	2.74

Adolescents have influence while buying family toiletries

140	Toothpaste/brush	96	136	80	48	40	400	1000	50	2.5
141	Soap bathing/face wash	24	112	104	80	80	400	1280	64	3.2
142	Shampoo	16	80	168	72	64	400	1288	64.4	3.22
143	Deodorant/perfumes	24	112	144	72	48	400	1208	60.4	3.02
144	Household cleaning products	24	168	96	56	56	400	1152	57.6	2.88
145	Cosmetics	56	136	128	48	32	400	1064	53.2	2.66

Adolescents have influence while buying family electronics

146	TV	16	96	232	48	8	400	1136	56.8	2.84
147	Refrigerator	88	104	80	72	56	400	1104	55.2	2.76
148	Telephones, mobile phones	96	152	48	40	64	400	1024	51.2	2.56
149	Video player, DVD	88	112	128	56	16	400	1000	50	2.5
150	Computer	48	144	104	48	56	400	1120	56	2.8

Adolescents have influence while buying family automobiles

151	Motorcycle	72	136	120	40	32	400	1024	51.2	2.56
152	Car	96	96	128	64	16	400	1008	50.4	2.52
153	Scooter	8	104	128	112	48	400	1288	64.4	3.22
154	Bicycle	16	96	144	112	32	400	1248	62.4	3.12

When your adolescent demands a product, you behave in the following manner

155	I ask my adolescent's opinion about product	56	144	72	72	56	400	1128	56.4	2.82
156	I set price and products boundaries	16	48	192	128	16	400	1280	64	3.2
157	I tell my adolescent the economic implication of the product	24	88	120	128	40	400	1272	63.6	3.18
158	I compromise on purchase options with my adolescent	24	136	112	104	24	400	1168	58.4	2.92

continued

Table 4.10 Continued

No.	Factors	No. of Respondents Scoring Points					Total No. of Responses (N)	Total Points Scored (TPS)**	Percent Points Score (PPS) $\frac{TPS}{5*N}$ 100	Central Tendency TPS/N
		A 1	B 2	C 3	D 4	E 5				
159	I make money deals or labour deals in exchange for his purchases	72	120	160	24	24	400	1008	50.4	2.52
160	I tell him to make the purchase in reward of good behaviour	48	80	208	24	40	400	1128	56.4	2.82
161	I give simple yes/no answer	16	192	80	80	32	400	1120	56	2.8
162	Ignore the request	48	168	64	80	40	400	1096	54.8	2.74
163	Postpone purchase	24	184	144	16	32	400	1048	52.4	2.62
164	Can't afford	24	176	120	48	32	400	1088	54.4	2.72
Following source is important for Product related information search										
165	Magazine	16	128	136	88	32	400	1192	59.6	2.98
166	Newspaper	48	160	128	24	40	400	1048	52.4	2.62
167	Internet	64	112	160	32	32	400	1056	52.8	2.64
168	TV	72	136	96	48	48	400	1064	53.2	2.66
169	Radio	56	168	64	56	56	400	1088	54.4	2.72
Following source is important for Leisure time										
170	Magazine	40	176	80	56	48	400	1096	54.8	2.74
171	Newspaper	80	64	112	112	32	400	1152	57.6	2.88
172	Internet	32	184	72	48	64	400	1128	56.4	2.82
173	TV	72	176	72	32	48	400	1008	50.4	2.52
174	Radio	80	112	144	32	32	400	1024	51.2	2.56
Following source is important for Information of current events										
175	Magazine	64	168	96	32	40	400	1016	50.8	2.54
176	Newspaper	24	144	160	40	32	400	1112	55.6	2.78
177	Internet	96	72	96	64	72	400	1144	57.2	2.86
178	TV	40	144	88	96	32	400	1136	56.8	2.84
179	Radio	88	144	80	48	40	400	1008	50.4	2.52

You give importance to different kinds of appeals and demonstrations present in TV advertisements

		A	B	C	D	E				TPS
180	Emotional appeal for creation of mood and emotions	16	200	72	64	48	400	1128	56.4	2.82
181	Rational appeal depicting taste, health and nutrient claims in the product	64	144	112	48	32	400	1040	52	2.6
182	Rational appeal depicting economy and savings in the purchase of product	32	88	160	32	88	400	1256	62.8	3.14
	Whether you agree or disagree to the following statements									
183	I get irritated when TV advertisements are there mid programme	72	120	104	24	80	400	1120	56	2.8
184	TV advertisements present true features of the product advertised	16	128	144	64	48	400	1200	60	3
185	I don't believe everything TV commercials tell me	104	136	72	32	56	400	1000	50	2.5
186	TV advertisements provide information about new products launched in the market	56	96	112	104	32	400	1160	58	2.9
187	I think TV advertisements are misleading as they only show good things about the product advertised	16	128	136	88	32	400	1192	59.6	2.98
188	When TV commercials are there I change the channel	48	160	128	24	40	400	1048	52.4	2.62

Note

$** \text{TPS} = A \times 1 + B \times 2 + C \times 3 + D \times 4 + E \times 5$

the observed variables load on different factors. Unrotated factor loadings are extremely hard to interpret, regardless of the extraction methods. Rotation helps in arriving at a simple pattern of factor loadings by maximizing high correlations and minimizing low ones. For a good factor solution, a particular variable should load high on one factor and low on all other factors in the rotated factor matrix. Researchers commonly use a cut-off of 0.40 to identify high loadings.

Rotation could be orthogonal or oblique. Orthogonal rotation should be used under the assumption that the underlying factors are uncorrelated with each other. However, if the researcher has theoretical reasons to believe that the factors may be correlated, oblique rotation is a better choice. Rotation is used to reduce the number of factors on which the variables under investigation have high loadings. Rotation makes the interpretation of the analysis easier and does not change anything. Values less than 0.55 are concealed. The variables are listed in the order of size of their factor loadings. After rotation, factor structure was clarified, as most of the variables loaded highly on to the components before rotation.

4.4.1 Results of Factor Analysis for Part A: Adolescents

Descriptive statistics of all the dimensions like mean and standard deviation are shown in Table 4.12.

Table 4.13 gives the correlation of each variable with one another.

The Eigen values with each linear component before extraction, after extraction and after rotation are listed in Table 4.14.

The communalities before and after extraction are listed in Table 4.15.

Before rotation, component 1, component 2, component 3, component 4 and component 5 contribute for 12.860%, 4.468%, 2.968%, 2.355% and 1.803% respectively, whereas after rotation component 1, component 2, component 3, component 4 and component 5 contribute for 8.510%, 5.776%, 4.113%, 3.649% and 2.406% respectively.

Communalities show the extent of the variance in the variables has been accounted for by the extracted factors. The component matrix contains the loading of each variable on to each factor. Table 4.16 shows the component matrix before rotation. In that table, loadings less than 0.55 are suppressed and as a result almost 50% of factors are suppressed.

Rotated component matrix is the matrix of the factor loadings for each variable on to each factor and is listed in Table 4.17. In that table, loadings less than 0.55 are suppressed and as a result almost 50% of factors are suppressed.

Only five components are extracted as a result of the factor analysis, which have been classified into dimensions. Each dimension is further divided into factors. The association of each factor with its dimension and component is listed in Table 4.18.

Table 4.11 Dimensions Surveyed from the Respondents

Father has the right	V1
Parents can impose	V2
Family member's ideas	V3
Younger generation more aware	V4
Parents allow you to buy	V5
Parents appreciate	V6
Parents dissatisfied	V7
Adolescents initiate and influence	V8
Self-concept	V9
Educated members	V10
Change in income	V11
Major part is spent by adolescents	V12
Buying costly products	V13
Problem recognizer	V14
Switch from brand	V15
Advertisements	V16
Promotional schemes	V17
Rapid growth	V18
Sources for personal consumable items	V19
Sources for personal durable items	V20
Sources for family toiletries	V21
Sources for family electronics	V22
Sources for family automobile	V23
Sources for other activities such as movie watching	V24
You influence personal consumable items	V25
You influence personal durable items	V26
You influence other activities such as movie watching	V27
Entertainment	V28
Homework	V29
Sports related information	V30
Cartoon	V31
Emotional appeal	V32
Your behaviour	V33
TV advertisement	V34

Table 4.12 Descriptive Statistics

	Mean	Standard Deviation	Analysis N
V1	3.240	0.9511	400
V2	2.680	1.0100	400
V3	2.780	0.9869	400
V4	2.560	1.0436	400
V5	2.600	1.3131	400
V6	2.780	1.2552	400
V7	3.240	1.1070	400
V8	2.640	1.2785	400
V9	2.660	1.1781	400
V10	2.360	1.0739	400
V11	2.720	1.0413	400
V12	2.480	1.0060	400
V13	3.140	1.0786	400
V14	3.300	1.0643	400
V15	2.560	1.1874	400
V16	2.720	1.3289	400
V17	2.540	1.0823	400
V18	2.460	0.9647	400
V19	2.844	0.5211	400
V20	2.792	0.6948	400
V21	2.572	0.6773	400
V22	2.852	0.6189	400
V23	2.800	0.4905	400
V24	2.680	0.6126	400
V25	2.724	0.7274	400
V26	2.790	0.6107	400
V27	2.690	0.5045	400
V28	2.772	0.5477	400
V29	2.736	0.7656	400
V30	2.840	0.6100	400
V31	2.656	0.5763	400
V32	2.860	0.5442	400
V33	2.718	0.5990	400
V34	2.735	0.5029	400

Table 4.13 Correlation Matrix

		V1	*V2*	*V3*	*V4*	*V5*	*V6*	*V7*
Correlation	V1	1.000	0.310	0.291	−0.075	0.045	−0.124	0.307
	V2	0.310	1.000	0.030	−0.058	−0.142	0.118	0.176
	V3	0.291	0.030	1.000	0.100	0.334	0.333	0.397
	V4	−0.075	−0.058	0.100	1.000	0.018	0.263	0.022
	V5	0.045	−0.142	0.334	0.018	1.000	0.153	0.135
	V6	−0.124	0.118	0.333	0.263	0.153	1.000	0.370
	V7	0.307	0.176	0.397	0.022	0.135	0.370	1.000
	V8	0.220	−0.043	0.446	0.061	0.272	0.150	0.571
	V9	0.162	0.094	0.470	0.041	0.080	0.275	0.432
	V10	0.033	0.402	0.245	0.195	−0.068	0.327	0.130
	V11	0.291	0.124	0.291	−0.261	0.035	0.183	0.441
	V12	0.194	0.191	0.329	−0.199	−0.067	0.211	0.436
	V13	0.163	0.115	0.349	−0.088	0.365	0.378	0.375
	V14	0.424	0.090	0.025	−0.007	−0.115	−0.116	0.160
	V15	0.129	−0.134	0.054	0.086	−0.319	−0.173	0.065
	V16	0.244	0.097	0.350	0.027	0.005	0.420	0.441
	V17	0.030	0.030	0.018	−0.162	0.054	−0.119	−0.159
	V18	−0.099	0.069	0.212	0.321	−0.044	0.051	−0.066
	V19	0.731	0.530	0.339	−0.119	0.161	0.076	0.343
	V20	0.130	0.036	0.687	0.438	0.577	0.711	0.623
	V21	0.297	0.239	0.597	−0.040	0.100	0.375	0.672
	V22	0.367	0.072	0.308	−0.045	−0.014	0.164	0.345
	V23	0.610	0.178	0.431	0.024	0.212	0.052	0.266
	V24	0.139	0.307	0.646	0.469	0.558	0.711	0.403
	V25	0.316	0.223	0.585	0.025	0.153	0.403	0.810
	V26	0.363	0.113	0.350	−0.093	−0.030	0.197	0.411
	V27	0.270	0.070	0.386	0.064	0.236	0.122	0.178
	V28	0.559	0.397	0.671	0.378	0.570	0.294	0.388
	V29	0.181	0.217	0.586	0.180	0.186	0.661	0.770
	V30	0.419	0.125	0.361	−0.155	−0.045	0.158	0.508
	V31	0.341	0.079	0.466	0.061	0.167	0.172	0.243
	V32	0.675	0.648	0.558	−0.100	0.132	0.234	0.430
	V33	0.225	0.172	0.634	0.199	0.402	0.637	0.743
	V34	0.374	0.060	0.337	0.021	0.010	0.086	0.254

continued

Table 4.13 Continued

		V8	V9	V10	V11	V12	V13	V14
Correlation	V1	0.220	0.162	0.033	0.291	0.194	0.163	0.424
	V2	−0.043	0.094	0.402	0.124	0.191	0.115	0.090
	V3	0.446	0.470	0.245	0.291	0.329	0.349	0.025
	V4	0.061	0.041	0.195	−0.261	−0.199	−0.088	−0.007
	V5	0.272	0.080	−0.068	0.035	−0.067	0.365	−0.115
	V6	0.150	0.275	0.327	0.183	0.211	0.378	−0.116
	V7	0.571	0.432	0.130	0.441	0.436	0.375	0.160
	V8	1.000	0.305	0.007	0.165	0.104	0.197	0.330
	V9	0.305	1.000	0.192	0.184	0.459	0.353	0.209
	V10	0.007	0.192	1.000	0.162	0.285	0.233	0.028
	V11	0.165	0.184	0.162	1.000	0.263	0.338	0.040
	V12	0.104	0.459	0.285	0.263	1.000	0.271	0.221
	V13	0.197	0.353	0.233	0.338	0.271	1.000	−0.002
	V14	0.330	0.209	0.028	0.040	0.221	−0.002	1.000
	V15	0.239	0.165	0.014	0.095	0.228	−0.234	0.343
	V16	0.200	0.259	0.099	0.262	0.461	0.489	0.102
	V17	0.054	0.034	0.126	0.117	0.001	−0.099	0.155
	V18	0.021	0.173	0.266	0.069	−0.021	−0.024	−0.252
	V19	0.144	0.266	0.287	0.437	0.266	0.310	0.323
	V20	0.484	0.413	0.262	0.224	0.224	0.467	−0.029
	V21	0.567	0.717	0.521	0.563	0.667	0.455	0.284
	V22	0.378	0.382	0.183	0.321	0.456	0.434	0.573
	V23	0.179	0.312	0.244	0.440	0.195	0.273	0.207
	V24	0.329	0.343	0.383	0.136	0.159	0.432	−0.061
	V25	0.673	0.672	0.446	0.586	0.477	0.463	0.252
	V26	0.348	0.449	0.233	0.343	0.659	0.440	0.544
	V27	0.114	0.303	0.281	0.397	0.146	0.255	0.052
	V28	0.375	0.315	0.290	0.169	0.148	0.366	0.131
	V29	0.644	0.678	0.487	0.345	0.451	0.472	0.191
	V30	0.368	0.477	0.247	0.598	0.681	0.467	0.568
	V31	0.261	0.365	0.298	0.347	0.251	0.355	0.228
	V32	0.187	0.301	0.301	0.444	0.407	0.298	0.125
	V33	0.564	0.631	0.448	0.461	0.501	0.651	0.139
	V34	0.296	0.351	0.219	0.356	0.351	0.193	0.467

		V15	*V16*	*V17*	*V18*	*V19*	*V20*	*V21*
Correlation	V1	0.129	0.244	0.030	−0.099	0.731	0.130	0.297
	V2	−0.134	0.097	0.030	0.069	0.530	0.036	0.239
	V3	0.054	0.350	0.018	0.212	0.339	0.687	0.597
	V4	0.086	0.027	−0.162	0.321	−0.119	0.438	−0.040
	V5	−0.319	0.005	0.054	−0.044	0.161	0.577	0.100
	V6	−0.173	0.420	−0.119	0.051	0.076	0.711	0.375
	V7	0.065	0.441	−0.159	−0.066	0.343	0.623	0.672
	V8	0.239	0.200	0.054	0.021	0.144	0.484	0.567
	V9	0.165	0.259	0.034	0.173	0.266	0.413	0.717
	V10	0.014	0.099	0.126	0.266	0.287	0.262	0.521
	V11	0.095	0.262	0.117	0.069	0.437	0.224	0.563
	V12	0.228	0.461	0.001	−0.021	0.266	0.224	0.667
	V13	−0.234	0.489	−0.099	−0.024	0.310	0.467	0.455
	V14	0.343	0.102	0.155	−0.252	0.323	−0.029	0.284
	V15	1.000	0.201	0.201	0.265	0.122	−0.121	0.249
	V16	0.201	1.000	−0.104	0.132	0.261	0.401	0.415
	V17	0.201	−0.104	1.000	−0.027	0.278	−0.117	0.108
	V18	0.265	0.132	−0.027	1.000	0.039	0.137	0.167
	V19	0.122	0.261	0.278	0.039	1.000	0.258	0.451
	V20	−0.121	0.401	−0.117	0.137	0.258	1.000	0.545
	V21	0.249	0.415	0.108	0.167	0.451	0.545	1.000
	V22	0.577	0.676	0.401	0.054	0.475	0.238	0.568
	V23	0.289	0.289	0.272	0.407	0.860	0.313	0.447
	V24	−0.205	0.328	−0.065	0.202	0.343	0.921	0.454
	V25	0.189	0.393	0.052	0.141	0.451	0.635	0.951
	V26	0.550	0.697	0.339	0.040	0.474	0.262	0.663
	V27	0.291	0.237	0.317	0.541	0.700	0.319	0.403
	V28	−0.105	0.259	−0.008	0.169	0.603	0.750	0.439
	V29	0.097	0.440	−0.021	0.132	0.335	0.775	0.873
	V30	0.534	0.528	0.137	0.023	0.507	0.258	0.769
	V31	0.399	0.544	0.479	0.430	0.643	0.354	0.501
	V32	−0.018	0.368	0.129	0.085	0.814	0.400	0.528
	V33	0.020	0.498	−0.027	0.135	0.405	0.859	0.865
	V34	0.652	0.507	0.494	0.319	0.634	0.218	0.517

continued

Table 4.13 Continued

		V22	V23	V24	V25	V26	V27	V28
Correlation	V1	0.367	0.610	0.139	0.316	0.363	0.270	0.559
	V2	0.072	0.178	0.307	0.223	0.113	0.070	0.397
	V3	0.308	0.431	0.646	0.585	0.350	0.386	0.671
	V4	−0.045	0.024	0.469	0.025	−0.093	0.064	0.378
	V5	−0.014	0.212	0.558	0.153	−0.030	0.236	0.570
	V6	0.164	0.052	0.711	0.403	0.197	0.122	0.294
	V7	0.345	0.266	0.403	0.810	0.411	0.178	0.388
	V8	0.378	0.179	0.329	0.673	0.348	0.114	0.375
	V9	0.382	0.312	0.343	0.672	0.449	0.303	0.315
	V10	0.183	0.244	0.383	0.446	0.233	0.281	0.290
	V11	0.321	0.440	0.136	0.586	0.343	0.397	0.169
	V12	0.456	0.195	0.159	0.477	0.659	0.146	0.148
	V13	0.434	0.273	0.432	0.463	0.440	0.255	0.366
	V14	0.573	0.207	−0.061	0.252	0.544	0.052	0.131
	V15	0.577	0.289	−0.205	0.189	0.550	0.291	−0.105
	V16	0.676	0.289	0.328	0.393	0.697	0.237	0.259
	V17	0.401	0.272	−0.065	0.052	0.339	0.317	−0.008
	V18	0.054	0.407	0.202	0.141	0.040	0.541	0.169
	V19	0.475	0.860	0.343	0.451	0.474	0.700	0.603
	V20	0.238	0.313	0.921	0.635	0.262	0.319	0.750
	V21	0.568	0.447	0.454	0.951	0.663	0.403	0.439
	V22	1.000	0.497	0.169	0.508	0.970	0.431	0.241
	V23	0.497	1.000	0.318	0.443	0.473	0.928	0.543
	V24	0.169	0.318	1.000	0.501	0.186	0.320	0.841
	V25	0.508	0.443	0.501	1.000	0.560	0.389	0.486
	V26	0.970	0.473	0.186	0.560	1.000	0.404	0.244
	V27	0.431	0.928	0.320	0.389	0.404	1.000	0.397
	V28	0.241	0.543	0.841	0.486	0.244	0.397	1.000
	V29	0.449	0.318	0.673	0.923	0.503	0.301	0.512
	V30	0.838	0.496	0.150	0.683	0.894	0.405	0.241
	V31	0.756	0.820	0.339	0.471	0.708	0.836	0.419
	V32	0.343	0.631	0.512	0.510	0.402	0.449	0.700
	V33	0.486	0.412	0.762	0.893	0.548	0.395	0.638
	V34	0.869	0.774	0.175	0.461	0.830	0.764	0.286

		V29	V30	V31	V32	V33	V34
Correlation	V1	0.181	0.419	0.341	0.675	0.225	0.374
	V2	0.217	0.125	0.079	0.648	0.172	0.060
	V3	0.586	0.361	0.466	0.558	0.634	0.337
	V4	0.180	−0.155	0.061	−0.100	0.199	0.021
	V5	0.186	−0.045	0.167	0.132	0.402	0.010
	V6	0.661	0.158	0.172	0.234	0.637	0.086
	V7	0.770	0.508	0.243	0.430	0.743	0.254
	V8	0.644	0.368	0.261	0.187	0.564	0.296
	V9	0.678	0.477	0.365	0.301	0.631	0.351
	V10	0.487	0.247	0.298	0.301	0.448	0.219
	V11	0.345	0.598	0.347	0.444	0.461	0.356
	V12	0.451	0.681	0.251	0.407	0.501	0.351
	V13	0.472	0.467	0.355	0.298	0.651	0.193
	V14	0.191	0.568	0.228	0.125	0.139	0.467
	V15	0.097	0.534	0.399	−0.018	0.020	0.652
	V16	0.440	0.528	0.544	0.368	0.498	0.507
	V17	−0.021	0.137	0.479	0.129	−0.027	0.494
	V18	0.132	0.023	0.430	0.085	0.135	0.319
	V19	0.335	0.507	0.643	0.814	0.405	0.634
	V20	0.775	0.258	0.354	0.400	0.859	0.218
	V21	0.873	0.769	0.501	0.528	0.865	0.517
	V22	0.449	0.838	0.756	0.343	0.486	0.869
	V23	0.318	0.496	0.820	0.631	0.412	0.774
	V24	0.673	0.150	0.339	0.512	0.762	0.175
	V25	0.923	0.683	0.471	0.510	0.893	0.461
	V26	0.503	0.894	0.708	0.402	0.548	0.830
	V27	0.301	0.405	0.836	0.449	0.395	0.764
	V28	0.512	0.241	0.419	0.700	0.638	0.286
	V29	1.000	0.538	0.410	0.440	0.932	0.370
	V30	0.538	1.000	0.562	0.428	0.609	0.723
	V31	0.410	0.562	1.000	0.418	0.476	0.906
	V32	0.440	0.428	0.418	1.000	0.492	0.409
	V33	0.932	0.609	0.476	0.492	1.000	0.398
	V34	0.370	0.723	0.906	0.409	0.398	1.000

Table 4.14(a) Total Variance

Component	Initial Eigen Values			Extraction Sums of Squared Loadings		
	Total	% of Variance	Cumulative %	Total	% of Variance	Cumulative %
1	12.860	37.823	37.823	12.860	37.823	37.823
2	4.468	13.140	50.963	4.468	13.140	50.963
3	2.968	8.729	59.692	2.968	8.729	59.692
4	2.355	6.927	66.619	2.355	6.927	66.619
5	1.803	5.303	71.922	1.803	5.303	71.922
6	1.588	4.671	76.593			
7	1.434	4.217	80.810			
8	1.216	3.577	84.386			
9	0.901	2.649	87.035			
10	0.780	2.293	89.328			
11	0.665	1.956	91.284			
12	0.627	1.844	93.127			
13	0.512	1.507	94.634			
14	0.437	1.285	95.919			
15	0.414	1.218	97.138			
16	0.308	0.907	98.045			
17	0.243	0.713	98.758			
18	0.208	0.612	99.370			
19	0.133	0.391	99.760			
20	0.081	0.240	100.000			
21	1.064E-013	1.187E-013	100.000			
22	1.038E-013	1.112E-013	100.000			
23	1.034E-013	1.100E-013	100.000			
24	1.020E-013	1.060E-013	100.000			
25	1.017E-013	1.050E-013	100.000			
26	1.010E-013	1.031E-013	100.000			
27	1.002E-013	1.005E-013	100.000			
28	−1.003E-013	−1.007E-013	100.000			
29	−1.007E-013	−1.020E-013	100.000			
30	−1.015E-013	−1.045E-013	100.000			
31	−1.023E-013	−1.068E-013	100.000			
32	−1.032E-013	−1.094E-013	100.000			
33	−1.038E-013	−1.112E-013	100.000			
34	−1.048E-013	−1.141E-013	100.000			

Table 4.14(b) Total Variance Rotated

Component	Rotation Sums of Squared Loadings		
	Total	% of Variance	Cumulative %
1	8.510	25.028	25.028
2	5.776	16.989	42.017
3	4.113	12.096	54.113
4	3.649	10.733	64.846
5	2.406	7.075	71.922
6			
7			
8			
9			
10			
11			
12			
13			
14			
15			
16			
17			
18			
19			
20			
21			
22			
23			
24			
25			
26			
27			
28			
29			
30			
31			
32			
33			
34			

Table 4.15 Communalities

	Initial	Extraction
V1	1.000	0.719
V2	1.000	0.672
V3	1.000	0.580
V4	1.000	0.440
V5	1.000	0.673
V6	1.000	0.600
V7	1.000	0.677
V8	1.000	0.593
V9	1.000	0.465
V10	1.000	0.578
V11	1.000	0.371
V12	1.000	0.602
V13	1.000	0.394
V14	1.000	0.507
V15	1.000	0.670
V16	1.000	0.424
V17	1.000	0.317
V18	1.000	0.675
V19	1.000	0.938
V20	1.000	0.960
V21	1.000	0.892
V22	1.000	0.874
V23	1.000	0.903
V24	1.000	0.905
V25	1.000	0.858
V26	1.000	0.898
V27	1.000	0.837
V28	1.000	0.879
V29	1.000	0.917
V30	1.000	0.904
V31	1.000	0.905
V32	1.000	0.875
V33	1.000	0.974
V34	1.000	0.976

Table 4.16 Component Matrix

	Component				
	1	*2*	*3*	*4*	*5*
V33	0.885				
V21	0.878				
V25	0.869				
V29	0.829				
V30	0.783				
V26	0.770				
V31	0.748				
V22	0.732				
V34	0.727				
V23	0.702				
V32	0.693				
V20	0.691	−0.640			
V19	0.690				
V3	0.679				
V7	0.672				
V28	0.671				
V27	0.625				
V9	0.619				
V16	0.601				
V13					
V12					
V11					
V8					
V24	0.634	−0.652			
V15		0.633			
V6					
V17					
V14					
V2					
V18					
V1					
V4					
V10					.605
V5					

Table 4.17 Rotated Component Matrix

	Component				
	1	2	3	4	5
V29	0.885				
V21	0.876				
V25	0.855				
V33	0.852				
V7	0.753				
V30	0.710				
V12	0.684				
V9	0.642				
V6					
V16					
V13					
V8					
V11					
V34		0.924			
V31		0.832			
V22		0.739			
V27		0.721			
V23		0.719			
V15		0.702			
V26	0.642	0.662			
V17					
V5			0.814		
V28			0.756		
V20			0.749		
V24			0.721		
V3					
V32				0.817	
V19				0.778	
V2				0.773	
V1				0.619	
V18					0.732
V10					
V14					
V4					

Table 4.18 Associated Factors

Component	Dimensions	Factors
1	Adolescents' behaviour	• Homework • Family toiletries • Influence on personal consumable items • Behaviour • Parents dissatisfied • Sports related information • Major part of family income spent by adolescents • Self-concept
2	Adolescents' activities	• TV advertisement • Cartoon • Family electronics • Influence on other activities such as movie watching • Family automobile • Switch from brand • Influence on personal durable items
3	Influence on adolescents	• Parents allow • Entertainment • Sources for personal durable items • Sources for other activities such as movie watching
4	Adolescents' expression	• Emotional appeal • Sources for personal consumable items • Parents impose • Father has right
5	Adolescents' market	• Rapid growth

4.4.2 Results of Factor Analysis for Part B: Parents

Descriptive statistics of all the dimensions like mean and standard deviation are shown in Table 4.20.

Table 4.21 gives the correlation of each variable with one another.

The Eigen values with each linear component before extraction, after extraction and after rotation is listed in Table 4.22.

Before rotation, component 1, component 2, component 3, component 4 and component 5 contribute for 10.687%, 4.303%, 2.587%, 2.484% and 2.024% respectively, whereas after rotation component 1, component 2, component 3, component 4 and component 5 contribute for 7.017%, 4.948%, 4.122%, 3.875% and 2.121% respectively. Communalities show the extent of the variance in the variables has been accounted for by the extracted factors. The communalities before and after extraction are listed in Table 4.23.

Table 4.24 shows the component matrix before rotation. In that table, loadings less than 0.55 are suppressed and as a result almost 50% of factors are suppressed.

Rotated component matrix is the matrix of the factor loadings for each variable on to each factor and is listed in Table 4.25.

The association of each factor with its dimension and component is listed in Table 4.26. Only five components are extracted as a result of the factor analysis, which have been classified into dimensions. Each dimension is further divided into factors.

Table 4.19 Dimensions Surveyed from the Respondents

Liberty of expression	V1
Advertisement	V2
Purchase decisions	V3
Adolescents' consent	V4
Routine decisions	V5
Mother's and adolescents' finance	V6
Adolescents oblige	V7
Actual buyers	V8
Adolescents' needs and desires	V9
Cinema	V10
Personal consumption	V11
Quick buying decisions	V12
Brand conscious	V13
Physical attributes of product	V14
Cultural shift	V15
Household income	V16
Adolescents' hurry decisions	V17
Adolescents as mediator	V18
Adolescents' information	V19
Final effect	V20
Influence for change	V21
Role models	V22
Activities influencing adolescents' behaviour	V23
Advertising media	V24
Family toiletries	V25
Family electronics	V26
Family automobiles	V27
Your behaviour when adolescents demand	V28
Product related information search	V29
Leisure time	V30
Information of current events	V31
Emotional appeal	V32
TV advertisements	V33

Table 4.20 Descriptive Statistics

	Mean	Standard Deviation	Analysis N
V1	3.240	0.9511	400
V2	2.680	1.0100	400
V3	2.780	0.9869	400
V4	2.560	1.0436	400
V5	2.600	1.3131	400
V6	2.780	1.2552	400
V7	3.240	1.1070	400
V8	2.640	1.2785	400
V9	2.660	1.1781	400
V10	2.360	1.0739	400
V11	2.720	1.0413	400
V12	2.480	1.0060	400
V13	3.140	1.0786	400
V14	3.300	1.0643	400
V15	2.560	1.1874	400
V16	2.720	1.3289	400
V17	2.540	1.0823	400
V18	2.460	0.9647	400
V19	2.920	0.9777	400
V20	2.640	1.1462	400
V21	2.740	0.8913	400
V22	3.240	0.9511	400
V23	2.680	0.6126	400
V24	2.748	0.6869	400
V25	2.750	0.5676	400
V26	2.816	0.5265	400
V27	2.7950	0.72148	400
V28	2.712	0.5740	400
V29	2.800	0.4905	400
V30	2.680	0.6126	400
V31	2.724	0.7274	400
V32	2.973	0.6964	400
V33	2.640	0.5880	400

Table 4.21 Correlation Matrix

		V1	V2	V3	V4	V5	V6	V7
Correlation	V1	1.000	0.310	0.291	−0.075	0.045	−0.124	0.307
	V2	0.310	1.000	0.030	−0.058	−0.142	0.118	0.176
	V3	0.291	0.030	1.000	0.100	0.334	0.333	0.397
	V4	−0.075	−0.058	0.100	1.000	0.018	0.263	0.022
	V5	0.045	−0.142	0.334	0.018	1.000	0.153	0.135
	V6	−0.124	0.118	0.333	0.263	0.153	1.000	0.370
	V7	0.307	0.176	0.397	0.022	0.135	0.370	1.000
	V8	0.220	−0.043	0.446	0.061	0.272	0.150	0.571
	V9	0.162	0.094	0.470	0.041	0.080	0.275	0.432
	V10	0.033	0.402	0.245	0.195	−0.068	0.327	0.130
	V11	0.291	0.124	0.291	−0.261	0.035	0.183	0.441
	V12	0.194	0.191	0.329	−0.199	−0.067	0.211	0.436
	V13	0.163	0.115	0.349	−0.088	0.365	0.378	0.375
	V14	0.424	0.090	0.025	−0.007	−0.115	−0.116	0.160
	V15	0.129	−0.134	0.054	0.086	−0.319	−0.173	0.065
	V16	0.244	0.097	0.350	0.027	0.005	0.420	0.441
	V17	0.030	0.030	0.018	−0.162	0.054	−0.119	−0.159
	V18	−0.099	0.069	0.212	0.321	−0.044	0.051	−0.066
	V19	0.258	0.096	0.480	−0.035	−0.009	0.116	0.129
	V20	0.411	−0.082	0.160	0.035	0.410	−0.083	0.195
	V21	−0.092	0.086	−0.088	−0.210	0.065	0.200	0.084
	V22	1.000	0.310	0.291	−0.075	0.045	−0.124	0.307
	V23	0.139	0.307	0.646	0.469	0.558	0.711	0.403
	V24	0.316	0.235	0.590	−0.043	0.184	0.434	0.788
	V25	0.328	0.076	0.367	0.068	−0.143	0.077	0.213
	V26	0.737	0.500	0.532	−0.067	0.288	0.157	0.441
	V27	0.057	0.034	0.486	0.492	0.580	0.742	0.614
	V28	0.373	0.180	0.518	−0.048	0.052	0.310	0.582
	V29	0.610	0.178	0.431	0.024	0.212	0.052	0.266
	V30	0.139	0.307	0.646	0.469	0.558	0.711	0.403
	V31	0.316	0.223	0.585	0.025	0.153	0.403	0.810
	V32	0.393	0.197	0.351	−0.145	0.098	0.238	0.485
	V33	0.322	0.019	0.399	0.079	0.029	0.083	0.220

continued

Table 4.21 Continued

		V8	V9	V10	V11	V12	V13	V14
Correlation	V1	0.220	0.162	0.033	0.291	0.194	0.163	0.424
	V2	−0.043	0.094	0.402	0.124	0.191	0.115	0.090
	V3	0.446	0.470	0.245	0.291	0.329	0.349	0.025
	V4	0.061	0.041	0.195	−0.261	−0.199	−0.088	−0.007
	V5	0.272	0.080	−0.068	0.035	−0.067	0.365	−0.115
	V6	0.150	0.275	0.327	0.183	0.211	0.378	−0.116
	V7	0.571	0.432	0.130	0.441	0.436	0.375	0.160
	V8	1.000	0.305	0.007	0.165	0.104	0.197	0.330
	V9	0.305	1.000	0.192	0.184	0.459	0.353	0.209
	V10	0.007	0.192	1.000	0.162	0.285	0.233	0.028
	V11	0.165	0.184	0.162	1.000	0.263	0.338	0.040
	V12	0.104	0.459	0.285	0.263	1.000	0.271	0.221
	V13	0.197	0.353	0.233	0.338	0.271	1.000	−0.002
	V14	0.330	0.209	0.028	0.040	0.221	−0.002	1.000
	V15	0.239	0.165	0.014	0.095	0.228	−0.234	0.343
	V16	0.200	0.259	0.099	0.262	0.461	0.489	0.102
	V17	0.054	0.034	0.126	0.117	0.001	−0.099	0.155
	V18	0.021	0.173	0.266	0.069	−0.021	−0.024	−0.252
	V19	0.153	0.272	0.314	0.234	0.121	0.296	0.254
	V20	0.226	0.206	0.024	0.201	0.011	0.187	0.302
	V21	−0.223	−0.065	−0.028	0.310	0.207	0.038	−0.277
	V22	0.220	0.162	0.033	0.291	0.194	0.163	0.424
	V23	0.329	0.343	0.383	0.136	0.159	0.432	−0.061
	V24	0.575	0.683	0.449	0.574	0.631	0.631	0.237
	V25	0.332	0.362	0.258	0.271	0.357	0.156	0.523
	V26	0.253	0.338	0.259	0.454	0.341	0.328	0.235
	V27	0.431	0.337	0.231	0.170	0.157	0.443	−0.044
	V28	0.539	0.629	0.406	0.505	0.639	0.502	0.477
	V29	0.179	0.312	0.244	0.440	0.195	0.273	0.207
	V30	0.329	0.343	0.383	0.136	0.159	0.432	−0.061
	V31	0.673	0.672	0.446	0.586	0.477	0.463	0.252
	V32	0.319	0.510	0.272	0.321	0.734	0.646	0.615
	V33	0.294	0.354	0.248	0.315	0.282	0.211	0.301

		V15	V16	V17	V18	V19	V20	V21
Correlation	V1	0.129	0.244	0.030	−0.099	0.258	0.411	−0.092
	V2	−0.134	0.097	0.030	0.069	0.096	−0.082	0.086
	V3	0.054	0.350	0.018	0.212	0.480	0.160	−0.088
	V4	0.086	0.027	−0.162	0.321	−0.035	0.035	−0.210
	V5	−0.319	0.005	0.054	−0.044	−0.009	0.410	0.065
	V6	−0.173	0.420	−0.119	0.051	0.116	−0.083	0.200
	V7	0.065	0.441	−0.159	−0.066	0.129	0.195	0.084
	V8	0.239	0.200	0.054	0.021	0.153	0.226	−0.223
	V9	0.165	0.259	0.034	0.173	0.272	0.206	−0.065
	V10	0.014	0.099	0.126	0.266	0.314	0.024	−0.028
	V11	0.095	0.262	0.117	0.069	0.234	0.201	0.310
	V12	0.228	0.461	0.001	−0.021	0.121	0.011	0.207
	V13	−0.234	0.489	−0.099	−0.024	0.296	0.187	0.038
	V14	0.343	0.102	0.155	−0.252	0.254	0.302	−0.277
	V15	1.000	0.201	0.201	0.265	0.177	0.207	−0.089
	V16	0.201	1.000	−0.104	0.132	0.060	0.144	0.142
	V17	0.201	−0.104	1.000	−0.027	0.079	0.335	0.229
	V18	0.265	0.132	−0.027	1.000	0.124	0.005	0.000
	V19	0.177	0.060	0.079	0.124	1.000	0.153	−0.185
	V20	0.207	0.144	0.335	0.005	0.153	1.000	−0.092
	V21	−0.089	0.142	0.229	0.000	−0.185	−0.092	1.000
	V22	0.129	0.244	0.030	−0.099	0.258	0.411	−0.092
	V23	−0.205	0.328	−0.065	0.202	0.218	0.178	0.038
	V24	0.138	0.503	0.017	0.097	0.350	0.249	0.057
	V25	0.724	0.514	0.411	0.375	0.512	0.375	−0.043
	V26	0.075	0.367	0.252	0.072	0.314	0.581	0.265
	V27	−0.164	0.363	−0.147	0.093	0.083	0.238	0.073
	V28	0.458	0.609	0.280	0.128	0.380	0.366	0.037
	V29	0.289	0.289	0.272	0.407	0.552	0.656	0.211
	V30	−0.205	0.328	−0.065	0.202	0.218	0.178	0.038
	V31	0.189	0.393	0.052	0.141	0.341	0.270	0.007
	V32	0.164	0.526	0.028	−0.151	0.340	0.256	−0.022
	V33	0.663	0.512	0.459	0.440	0.467	0.596	0.012

continued

Table 4.21 Continued

		V22	V23	V24	V25	V26	V27	V28
Correlation	V1	1.000	0.139	0.316	0.328	0.737	0.057	0.373
	V2	0.310	0.307	0.235	0.076	0.500	0.034	0.180
	V3	0.291	0.646	0.590	0.367	0.532	0.486	0.518
	V4	−0.075	0.469	−0.043	0.068	−0.067	0.492	−0.048
	V5	0.045	0.558	0.184	−0.143	0.288	0.580	0.052
	V6	−0.124	0.711	0.434	0.077	0.157	0.742	0.310
	V7	0.307	0.403	0.788	0.213	0.441	0.614	0.582
	V8	0.220	0.329	0.575	0.332	0.253	0.431	0.539
	V9	0.162	0.343	0.683	0.362	0.338	0.337	0.629
	V10	0.033	0.383	0.449	0.258	0.259	0.231	0.406
	V11	0.291	0.136	0.574	0.271	0.454	0.170	0.505
	V12	0.194	0.159	0.631	0.357	0.341	0.157	0.639
	V13	0.163	0.432	0.631	0.156	0.328	0.443	0.502
	V14	0.424	−0.061	0.237	0.523	0.235	−0.044	0.477
	V15	0.129	−0.205	0.138	0.724	0.075	−0.164	0.458
	V16	0.244	0.328	0.503	0.514	0.367	0.363	0.609
	V17	0.030	−0.065	0.017	0.411	0.252	−0.147	0.280
	V18	−0.099	0.202	0.097	0.375	0.072	0.093	0.128
	V19	0.258	0.218	0.350	0.512	0.314	0.083	0.380
	V20	0.411	0.178	0.249	0.375	0.581	0.238	0.366
	V21	−0.092	0.038	0.057	−0.043	0.265	0.073	0.037
	V22	1.000	0.139	0.316	0.328	0.737	0.057	0.373
	V23	0.139	1.000	0.509	0.136	0.501	0.888	0.359
	V24	0.316	0.509	1.000	0.452	0.553	0.559	0.878
	V25	0.328	0.136	0.452	1.000	0.434	0.074	0.781
	V26	0.737	0.501	0.553	0.434	1.000	0.344	0.570
	V27	0.057	0.888	0.559	0.074	0.344	1.000	0.364
	V28	0.373	0.359	0.878	0.781	0.570	0.364	1.000
	V29	0.610	0.318	0.437	0.639	0.807	0.229	0.531
	V30	0.139	1.000	0.509	0.136	0.501	0.888	0.359
	V31	0.316	0.501	0.960	0.452	0.539	0.564	0.835
	V32	0.393	0.268	0.750	0.519	0.453	0.282	0.810
	V33	0.322	0.208	0.446	0.930	0.537	0.162	0.729

		V29	*V30*	*V31*	*V32*	*V33*
Correlation	V1	0.610	0.139	0.316	0.393	0.322
	V2	0.178	0.307	0.223	0.197	0.019
	V3	0.431	0.646	0.585	0.351	0.399
	V4	0.024	0.469	0.025	−0.145	0.079
	V5	0.212	0.558	0.153	0.098	0.029
	V6	0.052	0.711	0.403	0.238	0.083
	V7	0.266	0.403	0.810	0.485	0.220
	V8	0.179	0.329	0.673	0.319	0.294
	V9	0.312	0.343	0.672	0.510	0.354
	V10	0.244	0.383	0.446	0.272	0.248
	V11	0.440	0.136	0.586	0.321	0.315
	V12	0.195	0.159	0.477	0.734	0.282
	V13	0.273	0.432	0.463	0.646	0.211
	V14	0.207	−0.061	0.252	0.615	0.301
	V15	0.289	−0.205	0.189	0.164	0.663
	V16	0.289	0.328	0.393	0.526	0.512
	V17	0.272	−0.065	0.052	0.028	0.459
	V18	0.407	0.202	0.141	−0.151	0.440
	V19	0.552	0.218	0.341	0.340	0.467
	V20	0.656	0.178	0.270	0.256	0.596
	V21	0.211	0.038	0.007	−0.022	0.012
	V22	0.610	0.139	0.316	0.393	0.322
	V23	0.318	1.000	0.501	0.268	0.208
	V24	0.437	0.509	0.960	0.750	0.446
	V25	0.639	0.136	0.452	0.519	0.930
	V26	0.807	0.501	0.539	0.453	0.537
	V27	0.229	0.888	0.564	0.282	0.162
	V28	0.531	0.359	0.835	0.810	0.729
	V29	1.000	0.318	0.443	0.340	0.767
	V30	0.318	1.000	0.501	0.268	0.208
	V31	0.443	0.501	1.000	0.598	0.448
	V32	0.340	0.268	0.598	1.000	0.398
	V33	0.767	0.208	0.448	0.398	1.000

Table 4.22(a) Total Variance

Component	Initial Eigen values			Extraction Sums of Squared Loadings		
	Total	% of Variance	Cumulative %	Total	% of Variance	Cumulative %
1	10.687	32.383	32.383	10.687	32.383	32.383
2	4.303	13.038	45.422	4.303	13.038	45.422
3	2.587	7.838	53.260	2.587	7.838	53.260
4	2.484	7.527	60.787	2.484	7.527	60.787
5	2.024	6.132	66.919	2.024	6.132	66.919
6	1.752	5.309	72.228			
7	1.326	4.018	76.246			
8	1.268	3.843	80.089			
9	1.192	3.611	83.700			
10	0.853	2.584	86.284			
11	0.812	2.461	88.745			
12	0.703	2.129	90.874			
13	0.552	1.673	92.547			
14	0.518	1.569	94.116			
15	0.445	1.348	95.464			
16	0.386	1.170	96.634			
17	0.322	0.975	97.610			
18	0.286	0.867	98.476			
19	0.225	0.682	99.158			
20	0.167	0.507	99.666			
21	0.110	0.334	100.000			
22	1.048E-013	1.146E-013	100.000			
23	1.022E-013	1.065E-013	100.000			
24	1.020E-013	1.059E-013	100.000			
25	1.005E-013	1.014E-013	100.000			
26	1.001E-013	1.003E-013	100.000			
27	-1.001E-013	-1.002E-013	100.000			
28	-1.002E-013	-1.006E-013	100.000			
29	-1.005E-013	-1.014E-013	100.000			
30	-1.009E-013	-1.027E-013	100.000			
31	-1.014E-013	-1.042E-013	100.000			
32	-1.023E-013	-1.071E-013	100.000			
33	-1.032E-013	-1.098E-013	100.000			

Table 4.22(b) Total Variance Rotated

Component	Rotation Sums of Squared Loadings		
	Total	% of Variance	Cumulative %
1	7.017	21.263	21.263
2	4.948	14.993	36.256
3	4.122	12.491	48.747
4	3.875	11.743	60.491
5	2.121	6.429	66.919
6			
7			
8			
9			
10			
11			
12			
13			
14			
15			
16			
17			
18			
19			
20			
21			
22			
23			
24			
25			
26			
27			
28			
29			
30			
31			
32			
33			

Table 4.23 Communalities

	Initial	Extraction
V1	1.000	0.808
V2	1.000	0.304
V3	1.000	0.551
V4	1.000	0.572
V5	1.000	0.542
V6	1.000	0.671
V7	1.000	0.656
V8	1.000	0.588
V9	1.000	0.476
V10	1.000	0.364
V11	1.000	0.468
V12	1.000	0.639
V13	1.000	0.489
V14	1.000	0.621
V15	1.000	0.737
V16	1.000	0.425
V17	1.000	0.314
V18	1.000	0.588
V19	1.000	0.303
V20	1.000	0.588
V21	1.000	0.547
V22	1.000	0.808
V23	1.000	0.941
V24	1.000	0.943
V25	1.000	0.935
V26	1.000	0.943
V27	1.000	0.907
V28	1.000	0.963
V29	1.000	0.900
V30	1.000	0.941
V31	1.000	0.832
V32	1.000	0.790
V33	1.000	0.931

Table 4.24 Component Matrix

	Component				
	1	*2*	*3*	*4*	*5*
V28	0.904				
V24	0.900				
V31	0.869				
V26	0.769				
V32	0.739				
V29	0.697				
V3	0.688				
V33	0.684				
V7	0.682				
V25	0.664				
V9	0.622				
V16					
V13					
V12					
V8					
V11					
V19					
V20					
V10					
V27	0.605	−0.698			
V30	0.637	−0.666			
V23	0.637	−0.666			
V6		−0.638			
V15		0.612			
V14					
V5					
V17					
V18					
V4					
V1				−0.612	
V22				−0.612	
V21					0.716
V2					

Table 4.25 Rotated Component Matrix

	Component				
	1	*2*	*3*	*4*	*5*
V24	0.897				
V28	0.843				
V32	0.841				
V31	0.812				
V12	0.756				
V7	0.726				
V9	0.620				
V16					
V13					
V11					
V23		0.919			
V30		0.919			
V27		0.879			
V5		0.634			
V6		0.627			
V4					
V3					
V1			0.870		
V22			0.870		
V26			0.754		
V20			0.660		
V29			0.646		
V33				0.852	
V25				0.817	
V15				0.697	
V18				0.670	
V17					
V19					
V10					
V21					0.735
V8					
V14					
V2					

Table 4.26 Associated Factors

Component	Dimensions	Factors
1	Adolescents' behaviour	• Advertising media • Behaviour when adolescents demand • Emotional appeal • Information of current events • Quick buying decisions • Adolescents oblige • Adolescents' needs and desires
2	Adolescents' activities	• Activities affecting adolescents' behaviour • Leisure time • Family automobiles • Routine decisions • Mother and adolescents' finance
3	Adolescents' expression	• Liberty of expression • Role models • Family electronics • Final effect • Product related information search
4	Adolescents' mediator	• TV advertisement • Family toiletries • Cultural shift • Adolescents as mediator
5	Influence on adolescents	• Influence for change

4.5 Analytical Hierarchy Process (AHP)

AHP is a multi-criteria decision making technique that organizes and analyses multiple criteria by structuring them into a hierarchy and, thus, assessing their relative importance. It also helps in comparison of alternatives for every criteria and defining ranks to the alternatives, as stated by DSS (Decision Support System) Resources. AHP is quite helpful in situations where the decision set involves multiple criteria with rating according to multiple value choice. It is based on matrices and their corresponding Eigen vectors for generating approximate values (Saaty, 1980, 1994).

It is a prescriptive and a descriptive model of decision-making. It is valid for thousands of applications and the results were used by and acceptable to the organizations (Saaty, 1994). Thus, presently, it is the most used multiple criteria decision making (MCDM) technique (Singh and Ahuja, 2012). AHP makes comparison of criteria or alternatives in a pair-wise mode. For this, AHP uses an absolute numbers scale, validated by decision problem and physical experiments.

AHP can be applied to following situations:

- Choice – choosing one alternative from a given set of alternatives, when there are multiple criteria involved.
- Ranking – putting alternatives in an order from most to least desirable or vice-versa.
- Prioritization – determining the relative importance of alternatives, as opposed to selecting only one or simply ranking them.
- Resource allocation – allocating resources between sets of alternatives.
- Benchmarking – comparing the processes in own organization with those of other best organizations.
- Quality management – deals with multidimensional aspects of quality improvement and quality.
- Conflict resolution – resolving disputes among parties having apparently incompatible goals or positions.

The applications of AHP to complex situations are in the thousands and produce results in problems involving selection, priority setting, resource allocation and planning among choices. Other areas included are total quality management, the Balanced Scorecard, quality function deployment, business process re-engineering and forecasting.

4.5.1 Comparison Scale for Pair-Wise Comparison

Pair-wise comparison is an important stage in AHP for determining priority values of attributes and provides a relative rating for alternatives.

A measurement scale provides the relative importance of each factor by providing numerical judgments corresponding to verbal ones. This scale is a discrete one and ranges from one to nine, with nine showing the highest importance of one factor over another, and one describing equal importance among two factors, as shown in Table 4.27 (Singh and Khamba, 2015).

4.5.2 Pair-Wise Comparison of Attributes

While comparing attributes, the significance of the jth sub-objective is calculated from the ith one. For this, according to the number of variables, as x in this study, a 7×7 matrix was prepared, and used the following procedure for filling:

1 In the matrix, the diagonal elements are kept 1.
2 Values in the upper triangular matrix were filled by using the data compiled through responses from various organizations.
3 For the lower triangular matrix, the upper diagonal values are reciprocated as $a_{ji} = 1 / a_{ij}$.

Table 4.27 Comparison Scale Used

Intensity	Definition	Explanation
1	Equal importance	Two factors contribute equally to the objective
3	Moderately more important	Experience and judgment favour one factor over another`
5	Strongly more important	Experience and judgment strongly favour one factor over another`
7	Very strongly more important	A factor is strongly favoured and its dominance demonstrated in practice
9	Extremely more important	The evidence of favouring one factor over another is of the highest possible order of affirmation
2, 4, 6, 8: intermediate values when compromise is needed		

Source: Singh and Khamba, 2015.

4.5.3 Analysis Using AHP

Analysis in AHP is done by squaring the pair-wise matrix and then squaring till the Eigen vectors calculated are same. When the two successive iterations are almost the same, further squaring and iterations will generate the same solution. Then check for Consistency Ratio (CR). CR is described as the comparison between random index (RI) and consistency index (CI).

$$CR = CI/RI \qquad (4.1)$$

If CR is less than 0.1, that is 10%, then judgments are considered to be consistent and acceptable. Table 4.28 gives RI values.

Table 4.28 Random Index

N	1	2	3	4	5	6	7	8	9	10	11	12	13	14	15
RI	0	0	0.58	0.89	1.12	1.24	1.32	1.41	1.45	1.49	1.52	1.54	1.56	1.58	1.59

4.5.4 Results of AHP for Advertising Media

The comparison matrix for different attributes is shown in Table 4.29.

Table 4.29 Pair-Wise Comparison Matrix

	TV Commercials	Newspaper Advertisement	Advertisements on Vehicles	Magazine Advertisement	Billboard Advertisement	Radio Advertisement	Browser Advertisement
TV Commercials	1	3	5	4	3	5	4
Newspaper Advertisement	0.333333	1	4	3	0.25	3	2
Advertisements on Vehicles	0.2	0.25	1	0.5	0.333333	2	0.333333
Magazine Advertisement	0.25	0.333333	2	1	0.333333	3	0.5
Billboard Advertisement	0.333333	4	3	3	1	3	0.5
Radio Advertisement	0.2	0.333333	0.5	0.333333	0.333333	1	0.333333
Browser Advertisement	0.25	0.5	3	2	2	3	1

The consistency test values are shown in Table 4.30. Number of comparisons = 4, CR = 9.0%, principal Eigen value = 7.727.

Table 4.30 Consistency Test Values

Maximum Eigen Value	CI	RI	CR
7.727	0.1188	1.32	0.090

Priorities

The resulting weights for the criteria based on the above pair-wise comparisons are given in Table 4.31.

Table 4.31 Priorities of Attributes

Category	Priority	Rank
TV commercials	35.0%	1
Newspaper advertisement	14.9%	3
Advertisements on vehicles	5.0%	6
Magazine advertisement	7.4%	5
Billboard advertisement	19.1%	2
Radio advertisement	4.2%	7
Browser advertisement	14.4%	4

4.5.5 Results of AHP for Importance of Activities

The comparison matrix for different attributes is shown in Table 4.32.

Table 4.32 Pair-Wise Comparison Matrix

	Entertainment	Homework	Listening to Music	Product Related Information Search	Sports Related Information	Leisure Time	Cartoon	Information on Current Events
Entertainment	1	3	2	4	3	2	3	0.25
Homework	0.333333	1	0.333333	0.5	0.5	0.25	0.333333	0.25
Listening to Music	0.5	3	1	3	0.5	2	0.333333	0.25
Product Related Information Search	0.25	2	0.333333	1	0.5	0.333333	0.333333	0.25
Sports Related Information	0.333333	2	2	2	1	0.333333	2	0.25
Leisure Time	0.5	4	0.5	3	3	1	2	0.333333
Cartoon	0.333333	3	3	3	0.5	0.5	1	0.333333
Information on Current Events	4	4	4	4	4	3	3	1

Table 4.33 Consistency Test Values

Maximum Eigen Value	CI	RI	CR
8.924	0.133	1.41	0.094

Table 4.34 Priorities from Attributes

Category	Priority (%)	Rank
Entertainment	17.9	2
Homework	3.9	8
Listening to music	9.6	5
Product related information search	4.5	7
Sports related information	9.4	6
Leisure time	12.9	3
Cartoon	10.3	4
Information on current events	31.6	1

The consistency test values are shown in Table 4.33.

Number of comparisons = 5, CR = 9.4%, principal Eigen value = 8.924.

Priorities

The resulting weights for the criteria based on the above pair-wise comparisons are given in Table 4.34.

4.6 Technique for Order of Preference by Similarity to Ideal Solution (TOPSIS)

TOPSIS was developed by Yoon (1980) and Hwang and Yoon (1981), for solving MCDM problems. This method is based on the idea that the chosen alternative should be farthest from the Negative Ideal Solution (NIS) and nearest to the Positive Ideal Solution (PIS). This is a more realistic form of modelling as compared to non-compensatory methods, in which alternative solutions are included or excluded according to hard cutoffs. For instance, NIS maximizes the cost and minimizes the benefit, whereas PIS maximizes the benefit and minimizes the cost. It assumes that each criterion requires being maximized or minimized. In this method, options are graded according to ideal solution similarity. An option has a higher grade if the option is more similar to an ideal solution. An ideal solution is a solution that is the best from any aspect. It assumes that we have m alternatives (options) and n attributes/criteria and we have the score of each option with respect to each criterion.

It is a technique for ranking different alternatives according to closeness to the ideal solution. The procedure is based on an intuitive and simple idea, that is, the optimal ideal solution, having the maximum benefit, is obtained by selecting the best alternative which is far from the most unsuitable alternative, having minimal benefits. The ideal solution should have a rank of one, while the worst alternative should have a rank approaching zero. This method considers three types of attributes or criteria:

- qualitative benefit attributes/criteria
- quantitative benefit attributes
- cost attributes or criteria.

In this method two artificial alternatives are hypothesized:

Ideal alternative: the one which has the best level for all attributes considered.
Negative ideal alternative: the one which has the worst attribute values.

Let X_{ij} score of option i with respect to criterion j. We have a matrix $X=(X_{ij})m \times n$ matrix. Let J be the set of benefit attributes or criteria (more is better) and J' be the set of negative attributes or criteria (less is better).
Step 1. Construct normalized decision matrix. Normalize scores or data as follows:

$$r_{ij}=X_{ij}/(\Sigma X^2_{ij}) \text{ for } i=1, \ldots, m; j=1, \ldots, n \qquad (4.2)$$

Step 2. Construct the weighted normalized decision matrix. Not all of the selection criteria may be of equal importance and hence weighting was introduced from the AHP technique to quantify the relative importance of the different selection criteria. An element of the new matrix is: $v_{ij}=w_j \, r_{ij}$.
Step 3. Determine the ideal and negative ideal solutions.
Ideal solution, $A^*=\{v_1^*, \ldots, v_n^*\}$, where

$$v_j^*=\{\max (v_{ij}) \text{ if } j \in J; \min (v_{ij}) \text{ if } j \in J'\} \qquad (4.3)$$

Negative ideal solution, $A'=\{v_1' \ldots, v_n'\}$, where

$$v'=\{\min (v_{ij}) \text{ if } j \in J; \max (v_{ij}) \text{ if } j \in J'\} \qquad (4.4)$$

Step 4. Calculate the separation measures for each alternative.
The separation from the ideal alternative is:

$$S_i^*=[\Sigma(v_j^*-v_{ij})^2]^{\frac{1}{2}} \, i=1, \ldots, m \qquad (4.5)$$

Similarly, the separation from the negative ideal alternative is:

$$S_i' = [\Sigma(v_j' - v_{ij})^2]^{1/2} \; i = 1, \ldots, m \tag{4.6}$$

Step 5. Calculate the relative closeness to the ideal solution C_i^*

$$C_i^* = S_i' / (S_i^* + S_i'), \; 0 < C_i^* < 1 \tag{4.7}$$

Select the option with C_i^* closest to one.

4.6.1 Results of TOPSIS for Advertising Media

Table 4.35 shows the decision matrix for TOPSIS.
Table 4.36 shows the ranking from TOPSIS.

4.6.2 Results of TOPSIS for Importance of Activities

Table 4.37 shows the decision matrix for TOPSIS.
Table 4.38 shows the ranking from TOPSIS.

4.7 VIKOR Method

The compromise solution is a feasible solution that is the closest to the ideal solution, and a compromise means an agreement established by mutual concession. The compromise solution method, also known as (VIKOR) the *Vlse Kriterijumska Optimizacija I KOmpromisno Resenje* in Serbian, which means multi-criteria optimization (MCO) and compromise solution, introduced as one applicable technique to implement within multi-attribute decision making. It focuses on ranking and selecting from a set of alternatives in the presence of conflicting criteria.

The compromise solution, whose foundation was established by Yu (1973) and Zelrny (1973) is a feasible solution, which is the closest to the ideal, and here "compromise" means an agreement established by mutual concessions. The VIKOR method determines the compromise ranking list and the compromise solution by introducing the multi-criteria ranking index based on the particular measure of "closeness" to the "ideal" solution.

The procedure of VIKOR for ranking alternatives is as follows:

Step 1. Determine that best X_j^* and the worst X_j^- values of all criterion functions, where $j = 1, 2, \ldots, n$.
Step 2. Range Standardized Decision Matrix

$$X_{ij}' = [(X_{ij} - X_j^-) / (X_j^* - X_j^-)] \tag{4.8}$$

Table 4.35 Decision Matrix for TOPSIS

	TV Commercials	Newspaper Advertisement	Advertisements on Vehicles	Magazine Advertisement	Billboard Advertisement	Radio Advertisement	Browser Advertisement
TV Commercials	1	3	5	4	3	5	4
Newspaper Advertisement	0.333333	1	4	3	0.25	3	2
Advertisements on Vehicles	0.2	0.25	1	0.5	0.333333	2	0.333333
Magazine Advertisement	0.25	0.333333	2	1	0.333333	3	0.5
Billboard Advertisement	0.333333	4	3	3	1	3	0.5
Radio Advertisement	0.2	0.333333	0.5	0.333333	0.333333	1	0.333333
Browser Advertisement	0.25	0.5	3	2	2	3	1

Table 4.36 Ranking from TOPSIS

Category	Si*	Si'	Si* + Si'	Ci = Si'/Si* + Si'	Rank
TV commercials	0.071633	0.085815	0.157448	0.545037092	1
Newspaper advertisement	0.094622	0.057902	0.152524	0.379625502	3
Advertisements on vehicles	0.067459	0.034597	0.102056	0.339000157	6
Magazine advertisement	0.098658	0.042902	0.14156	0.303065838	5
Billboard advertisement	0.074352	0.078052	0.152404	0.512138789	2
Radio advertisement	0.071455	0.035549	0.107004	0.332221225	7
Browser advertisement	0.088109	0.040103	0.128212	0.312786635	4

Table 4.37 Decision Matrix for TOPSIS

	Entertainment	Homework	Listening to Music	Product Related Information Search	Sports Related Information	Leisure Time	Cartoon	Information on Current Events
Entertainment	1	3	2	4	3	2	3	0.25
Homework	0.333333	1	0.333333	0.5	0.5	0.25	0.333333	0.25
Listening to Music	0.5	3	1	3	0.5	2	0.333333	0.25
Product Related Information Search	0.25	2	0.333333	1	0.5	0.333333	0.333333	0.25
Sports Related Information	0.333333	2	2	2	1	0.333333	2	0.25
Leisure Time	0.5	4	0.5	3	3	1	2	0.333333
Cartoon	0.333333	3	3	3	0.5	0.5	1	0.333333
Information on Current Events	4	4	4	4	4	3	3	1

Table 4.38 Ranking from TOPSIS

Category	Si^*	Si'	$Si^* + Si'$	$Ci = Si'/Si^* + Si'$	Rank
Entertainment	0.076832	0.065397	0.142229	0.459798	2
Homework	0.088229	0.035458	0.123687	0.286672	8
Listening to music	0.080399	0.056481	0.13688	0.412632	5
Product related information search	0.089101	0.036424	0.125524	0.290172	7
Sports related information	0.082686	0.051385	0.134071	0.383267	6
Leisure time	0.080475	0.059933	0.140409	0.42685	3
Cartoon	0.079631	0.059219	0.13885	0.426496	4
Information on current events	0.073511	0.065247	0.138758	0.470221	1

Step 3. Compute the S_i (the maximum utility) and R_i (the minimum regret) values, $i = 1, 2, ..., m$ by the relations:

$$S_i = \sum W_j^*(X_j^* - X_{ij})/(X_j - X_j^-) \tag{4.9}$$

$$R_i = \max[\sum W_j^*(X_j^* - X_{ij})/(X_j - X_j^-)] \tag{4.10}$$

Where w_j is the weight of the jth criterion which expresses the relative importance of criteria.

Coefficient of Variation

The weight of the criterion reflects its importance in MCDM. Range standardization was done to transform different scales and units among various criteria into common measurable units in order to compare their weights.

$$X'_{ij} = [(X_{ij} - \min X_{ij})/(\max X_{ij} - \min X_{ij})]$$

$D' = (x')_{m \times n}$ is the matrix after range standardization; max x_{ij}, min x_{ij} are the maximum and the minimum values of the criterion (j) respectively, all values in D' are ($0 \leq x'_{ij} \leq 1$). So, according to the normalized matrix, $D' = (x')_{m \times n}$

The Standard Deviation (σ_j) calculated for every criterion independently as:

$$\sigma_j = \sqrt{1/m \sum (X'_{ij} - X'_j)^2} \tag{4.11}$$

Where X'_j is the mean of the values of the jth criterion after normalization and $j = 1, 2, ..., n$.

After calculating (σ_j) for all criteria, the CV of the criterion (j) will be as shown:

$$CV_j = \sigma_j / X'j \tag{4.12}$$

The weight (W_j) of the criterion (j) can be defined as

$$W_j = CV_j / \sum CV_j \tag{4.13}$$

Where $j = 1, 2, ..., n$.

Step 4. Compute the value Q_i, $i = 1, 2, ..., m$, by the relation

$$Q_i = \{v(S_i - S^*)/S^- - S^*)\} + \{(1-v)(R_i - R^*)/R^- - R^*)\} \tag{4.14}$$

Where $S^* = \min S_i$, $S^- = \max S_i$, $R^* = \min R_i$, $R^- = \max R_i$ and v is the introduced weight of the strategy of S_i and R_i.

Step 5. Rank the alternatives, sorting by the S, R and Q values in decreasing order.

4.7.1 Results of VIKOR for Advertising Media

Table 4.39 shows the decision matrix.

Table 4.39 Decision Matrix

	TV Commercials	Newspaper Advertisement	Advertisements on Vehicles	Magazine Advertisement	Billboard Advertisement	Radio Advertisement	Browser Advertisement
TV Commercials	1	3	5	4	3	5	4
Newspaper Advertisement	0.333333	1	4	3	0.25	3	2
Advertisements on Vehicles	0.2	0.25	1	0.5	0.333333	2	0.333333
Magazine Advertisement	0.25	0.333333	2	1	0.333333	3	0.5
Billboard Advertisement	0.333333	4	3	3	1	3	0.5
Radio Advertisement	0.2	0.333333	0.5	0.333333	0.333333	1	0.333333
Browser Advertisement	0.25	0.5	3	2	2	3	1

Table 4.40 Weights Assigned to Criteria

Category	x_j	sig_j	CV_j	W_j
TV commercials	0.208333	0.329404	1.58114	0.208
Newspaper advertisement	0.292063	0.375329	1.285094	0.169055
Advertisements on vehicles	0.47619	0.32915	0.691215	0.09093
Magazine advertisement	0.448553	0.357113	0.796145	0.104733
Billboard advertisement	0.285714	0.360687	1.262404	0.16607
Radio advertisement	0.464286	0.281215	0.605693	0.079679
Browser advertisement	0.247437	0.341448	1.379937	0.181532

Table 4.41 Ranking List and Scores

Category	Si	Ri	Qi	$Rank$
TV commercials	0.093282	0.078473	0	1
Newspaper advertisement	0.333548	0.09541	0.266811	3
Advertisements on vehicles	0.659657	0.159017	0.809721	6
Magazine advertisement	0.625485	0.138778	0.692423	5
Billboard advertisement	0.292322	0.084809	0.186784	2
Radio advertisement	0.720828	0.19082	1	7
Browser advertisement	0.435333	0.134398	0.521425	4

Table 4.40 provides the weights assigned to criteria. The results are shown in Table 4.41.

4.7.2 *Results of VIKOR for Advertising Media*

Table 4.42 shows the decision matrix.

Table 4.42 Decision Matrix

	Entertainment	Homework	Listening to Music	Product Related Information Search	Sports Related Information	Leisure Time	Cartoon	Information on Current Events
Entertainment	1	3	2	4	3	2	3	0.25
Homework	0.333333	1	0.333333	0.5	0.5	0.25	0.333333	0.25
Listening to Music	0.5	3	1	3	0.5	2	0.333333	0.25
Product Related Information Search	0.25	2	0.333333	1	0.5	0.333333	0.333333	0.25
Sports Related Information	0.333333	2	2	2	1	0.333333	2	0.25
Leisure Time	0.5	4	0.5	3	3	1	2	0.333333
Cartoon	0.333333	3	3	3	0.5	0.5	1	0.333333
Information on Current Events	4	4	4	4	4	3	3	1

Table 4.43 provides the weights assigned to criteria. The results are shown in Table 4.44.

Table 4.43 Weights Assigned to Criteria

Category	x_j	sig_j	CV_j	W_j
Entertainment	0.882812	0.525835	0.595636	0.152013
Homework	0.666667	0.091287	0.136931	0.034946
Listening to music	0.25463	0.099389	0.390327	0.099616
Product related information search	0.608311	0.116596	0.191672	0.048917
Sports related information	0.5	0.17531	0.350619	0.089482
Leisure time	0.044271	0.085299	1.926752	0.491728
Cartoon	0.318801	0.104055	0.326394	0.083299
Information on current events	0.205729	0.107274	0.521432	0.133075

Table 4.44 Ranking List and Scores

Category	Si	Ri	Qi	$Rank$
Entertainment	0.305974	0.078473	0.32299	2
Homework	0.599292	0.178641	1	8
Listening to usic	0.556109	0.095991	0.607286	5
Product related information search	0.591051	0.142913	0.838934	7
Sports related information	0.570648	0.122845	0.412614	6
Leisure time	0.334727	0.093681	0.594227	3
Cartoon	0.542396	0.095616	0	4
Information on current events	0	0.062783	0.735308	1

5 Conclusions and Future Scope of Work

In previous chapters, data analysis and hypotheses testing has been presented. This chapter starts by presenting the summary of this research, followed by the contributions from the research. Then, the research limitations are presented and at last, scope for future works is outlined.

5.1 Summary of Study

The study was aimed at identifying the role of adolescents in Indian urban families. The study also critically examined adolescents' role in influencing buying decision making. The major objective of this research was to examine adolescents' behaviour, thus, their role in decision making. Lastly, the research culminated by ranking various issues that affect adolescents' decision making. Primarily, the focus of this research was to determine the role that adolescents play in buying decision making when viewed from an Indian urban family's perception. This chapter presents the conclusions and recommendations for the future from this study.

After reviewing more than 150 papers, it was observed that the role of adolescents in family buying decision making had not yet been addressed. Based on the research gaps, the objectives were framed and issues for the study were listed along with the methodology adopted for the research work.

During this research work, a questionnaire was prepared for the survey to be conducted in the Punjab, Chandigarh and Haryana. For the questionnaire a pilot survey was made for finalizing the questionnaire. During the pilot survey, academicians and existing literature were consulted. Responses to the questionnaire were received from $400 \times 2 = 800$ respondents (one from adolescents and one from parents of same unit: Punjab-150, Chandigarh-100 and Haryana-150).

After completing the survey, preliminary analysis of the data was carried out. First, Cronbach alpha, a reliability analysis, was performed to analyse the prepared questionnaire. After reliability analysis, demographic data was analysed by applying t-test, chi-square and ANOVA (F-test). Then various quantitative techniques were employed like PPS and central tendency. This was followed by FA, which also included correlation of the above data. Based on the data analysis, factors were selected for detailed study in various manufacturing units. Then it was followed by qualitative analysis of the data. First, AHP, followed by TOPSIS and VIKOR.

5.2 Research Implications

The research highlights the attributes of adolescents in family buying decision making. Moreover, the study illustrates the relationship of adolescents and parents in Indian urban families while buying. The research critically examines the impact that adolescents have. This study is a legitimate reaction to a developing need of both academicians and professionals for better comprehension of the relationship of adolescents in buying decision making.

The empirical analysis was conducted in this research to evaluate the critical contribution of adolescents in decision making. The association amongst adolescents and parents has been deployed to critically examine the impact of adolescents in buying decision making. The conclusions drawn from the research work have been highlighted below.

5.2.1 Reliability Analysis

According to the response from the respondents, the value of Cronbach alpha came to be 0.975 for the overall questionnaire as shown in Table 4.1.

5.2.2 Demographic Analysis

5.2.2.1 Gender

Of the total respondents, 58% were males and 42% were females. A similar pattern was also depicted when compared with state-wise data: there were 57.3% males from Punjab, 53% males from Chandigarh and 62% males from Haryana. The mean male respondents were 77.33 and females were 56. The mean data was statistically at par as indicated by the t-value of 1.60 and even chi-square value of 2.03 also indicated the same. Similar results have been given by ANOVA (f-test) as f-value comes out to be 1.01792 and corresponding p-value of 0.459.

5.2.2.2 Education

Of the respondents, 38.75% of the total were from schools and 61.25% were from college. A similar pattern was also depicted when comparing state-wise data: there were 43.3%, 37% and 35.3% from schools of Punjab, Chandigarh and Haryana, respectively. The mean respondents from schools were 51.67 and colleges were 81.67. The mean data was statistically at par as indicated by the t-value of -2.33 and even chi-square value of 2.19 also indicated the same. Similar results have been given by ANOVA (f-test) as f-value comes out to be 0.83001 and corresponding p-value of 0.516534.

5.2.2.3 Age

The average age of the total respondents was 14.99. A similar pattern was also depicted when comparing state-wise data: the average age for Punjab, Chandigarh and Haryana was 14.64, 15.15 and 15.24, respectively. Similar results have been given by ANOVA (f-test) as f-value comes out to be 2.771 and corresponding p-value of 0.63778.

5.2.2.4 Father's Qualification

Of the total respondents, 28.5% were matric pass, 36.9% were graduate and 34.5% were post-graduate. A similar pattern was also depicted when comparing state-wise data: there were 26.66%, 21% and 35% matric pass Punjab, Chandigarh and Haryana, respectively. The mean male respondents were 38 matric pass, 49.33 graduate and 46 post-graduate. The mean data was statistically at par as indicated by chi-square value of 2.2739. Similar results have been given by ANOVA (f-test) as f-value comes out to be 2.3855 and corresponding p-value of 0.172857.

5.2.2.5 Father's Occupation

Of the total respondents, 39% were businessmen, 48% were in service and 13% responded N.A. A similar pattern was also depicted when comparing state-wise data: there were 37.33%, 50.66% and 12% businessmen, in service and N.A., respectively in respondents from Punjab. The mean businessmen respondents were 52 and 64 in service. The mean data was statistically at par as indicated by chi-square value of 0.8889. Similar results have been given by ANOVA (f-test) as f-value comes out to be 0.45257 and corresponding p-value of 0.656049.

5.2.2.6 *Mother's Qualification*

Of the total respondents, 19.98% were matric pass, 44.74% were graduate and 36.24% were post-graduate. A similar pattern was also depicted when comparing state-wise data: there were 12.66%, 46% and 41.33% matric pass, graduate and post-graduate from Punjab respectively. The mean male respondents were 25.33 matric pass, 59.66 graduate and 48.33 post-graduate. The mean data was statistically at par as indicated by chi-square value of 1.8761. Similar results have been given by ANOVA (*f*-test) as *f*-value comes out to be 0.65963 and corresponding *p*-value of 0.550874.

5.2.2.7 *Mother's Occupation*

Of the total respondents, 54% were in service and 46% were housewives. A similar pattern was also depicted when comparing state-wise data: there were 54.49% and 45.49% in service and housewives, respectively in respondents from Punjab. The mean service women respondents were 72.66 and 60.66 were housewives. The mean data was statistically at par as indicated by *t*-value of 0.98 and even chi-square value of 1.84 also indicated the same. Similar results have been given by ANOVA (*f*-test) as *f*-value comes out to be 4.46429 and corresponding *p*-value of 0.126124.

5.2.2.8 *Annual Income*

Of the total respondents, 16.24% had income up to 2 Lakhs, 28.50% had income of 2–5 Lakhs, 38.75% had income of 5–10 Lakhs and 18.67% had income above 10 lakhs. A similar pattern was also depicted when comparing state-wise data: there were 14%, 25.33%, 42% and 18.67% had income up to 2 Lakhs, 2–5 Lakhs, 5–10 Lakhs and above 10 Lakhs, respectively, in respondents from Punjab. The mean respondents having income up to 2 Lakhs were 21.66, 2–5 Lakhs were 38, 5–10 Lakhs were 51.66 and above 10 Lakhs were 22. The mean data was statistically at par as indicated by chi-square value of 5.4799. Similar results have been given by ANOVA (*f*-test) as *f*-value comes out to be 0.88277 and corresponding *p*-value of 0.446612.

5.2.3 *PPS Results*

The research provides an insight into exploits of adolescents regarding their role in family buying decision making and provides an assessment of the prevailing status of Indian urban families. The average PPS for the whole questionnaire is 55.46809 and central tendency is 2.773404.

5.2.4 FA

The research has highlighted the role of adolescents in buying decision making in Indian urban families. The data analysis was conducted in this research to evaluate the impact that adolescents have in Indian families. The association of each factor with its dimensions and components are listed in Tables 4.18 and 4.26 for adolescents and parents, respectively. Only five components are extracted as a result of the FA, which have been classified into dimensions. Each dimension is further divided into factors. These components may be reviewed by managers as a productive result in increasing their sales, profit and building good relationships with their customers.

5.2.5 Results of Preliminary Data Analysis

The empirical analysis has highlighted different issues from adolescents' and parents' points of view, which are listed as follows.

From adolescents' viewpoint:
1 Adolescents' behaviour
   - Homework
   - Family toiletries
   - Influence on personal consumable items
   - Behaviour
   - Parents dissatisfied
   - Sports related information
   - Major part of family income spent by adolescents
   - Self-concept
2 Adolescents' activities
   - TV advertisement
   - Cartoon
   - Family electronics
   - Influence on other activities such as movie watching
   - Family automobile
   - Switch from brand
   - Influence on personal durable items
3 Influence on adolescents
   - Parents allow
   - Entertainment
   - Sources for personal durable items
   - Sources for other activities such as movie watching
4 Adolescents' expression
   - Emotional appeal

- Sources for personal consumable items
- Parents impose
- Father has right
5 Adolescents' market
- Rapid growth.

From parents' viewpoint
1 Adolescents' behaviour
- Advertising media
- Behaviour when adolescents demand
- Emotional appeal
- Information of current events
- Quick buying decisions
- Adolescents oblige
- Adolescents' needs and desires
2 Adolescents' activities
- Activities affecting adolescents' behaviour
- Leisure time
- Family automobiles
- Routine decisions
- Mother and adolescents' finance
3 Adolescents' expression
- Liberty of expression
- Role models
- Family electronics
- Final effect
- Product related information search
4 Adolescents' mediator
- TV advertisement
- Family toiletries
- Cultural shift
- Adolescents as mediator
5 Influence on adolescents
- Influence for change.

5.2.6 *Qualitative Analysis Results*

For parameter selection from the questionnaire, after analysis has been made using AHP. CR was computed as the ratio of CI and Random Consistency Index. For the study, the value of CR was obtained as less than 0.1 (9% and 9.4%), which means the judgments considered for the study were consistent and acceptable. Further, to validate the ranking as achieved from AHP, TOPSIS and VIKOR were employed and similar results were obtained.

5.3 Major Findings of the Study

This research is a legitimate reaction to the developing needs of adolescents in Indian urban families. Adolescents are effectively fitting into the consumer role owing to time pressures and income effects in dual career families. Moreover, exposure to mass media and discussions with parents ensure that adolescents are not only aware of the new brands available, but also know how to evaluate them on various parameters. An analysis of adolescents as consumers helps in the formulation of marketing strategies by identifying the motivations, interests and attitudes of adolescents who show the greatest involvement in making purchases in a specific product category. It has been seen that they act as purchasing agents for the family and are delegated the task of purchasing products which they themselves do not consume. Products for which adolescents act as purchasing agents should be identified to help marketers understand the features that are preferred by these purchasers and to help direct appropriate messages towards them.

The complexity of the factors typical to the Indian marketing environment such as the prevalence of a joint/extended family system, gifts of durables as dowry, etc., means that studies need to be designed more systematically to capture the effects of all variables important in the Indian family context. Individuals in rural settings in India subscribe to an extended family system and enter into and exit from extended households according to their needs and requirements throughout life. In this region, wives have been seen to exercise covert influence in domestic decisions on critical matters. With their acceptance of the role of breadwinner for the family, they may express themselves more openly and their husbands may increasingly accept their wife's informal power suggesting that shifts in family type occur over the life cycle of an individual both in India as well as in the West.

Adolescents in India may not have the purchasing power comparable to their Western counterparts, but they are still the centre of the universe in the Indian family system, and they can actually pull the parents to visit a place time and again. Adolescents are an enormously powerful medium for relationship building in India. They not only influence markets in terms of parental decision making to buy certain kinds of products, they are also future consumers. Hence more investigation of adolescents' roles in family decision making is imperative. The following are the statements accepted from the study.

The Statements Accepted

1 Adolescents are highly affected by physical attributes of a product.
2 Adolescents want liberty of their expressions.
3 Adolescents ambitions are materialistic in nature.
4 Cultural shift has brought about a change in the decision making process.
5 Adolescents are highly brand conscious.
6 Adolescents make quick buying decisions.
7 The father has a right to accept or reject any purchase decision at any time.
8 When personal consumption is individual, the other family members do not take part in the decision.
9 Family members are egoistic about their self-concept in purchase matters.
10 Change in income causes change in buying behaviour.
11 The increasing use of TV and cinema affects the decision making role of adolescents.
12 Role models are important in adolescents' buying decisions.
13 The internet and other technologies influence adolescents' buying behaviour.
14 The purchase decision in a family is taken as one entity.
15 Educated members play an effective role in the decision making process.

Thus, the following basic conclusions are drawn from the study:

1 Adolescents today have more autonomy and decision making power within the family than previous generations; they are emerging as influencers in household buying decisions. They are growing not only in size but also in influence as they are playing different buying roles in the household sector. They act as initiators, information seekers, influencers, deciders, buyers and actual users. They also act as purchasing agents for parents and play a role of mediator whenever there is any disagreement between the father and the mother about the purchase of any household product.
2 The size of the adolescents' market is growing as results show that both parents and adolescents agree in majority that there is rapid growth of market for adolescents' products over the past few years. Marketers are targeting consumers by using adolescents not only in the case of products meant for adolescents but also for the products used or purchased in the household sector. Adolescents are not only making their own buying decisions but also play a vital role in other

buying decisions of the products to be used or purchased in the household sector.

3   Media in its various manifestations has been able to carve out a niche for its advertisements in the heads and hearts of adolescents. Adolescents with their instant grasping power give valuable suggestions to their parents when they intend buying a particular item. Parents rely more upon the information provided by them, as they feel that adolescents have the latest information regarding the product.

4   Income has a great impact on the buying decision making process. The number of working women is increasing fast, which enhances the earnings of the household. It increases their propensity to consume. To reap the benefits of increase in income and better standards of living, the parents prefer to have fewer adolescents in their family without giving any special consideration to the gender of an adolescent.

5   Education also affects the buying decisions of respondents. It has helped in bringing openness in the family environment. Family members give due consideration to the price of a product and spend wisely at the marketplace.

6   Today's parents strongly desire to prepare their adolescent for adulthood or at least for self-sufficiency. This desire takes the form of providing skills to the youngsters so that they may cope with a rapidly changing economic scenario without the assistance of parents. Being a consumer is one of these skills. It seems clear that adolescents are being turned into consumers at a very early age through desires and with the encouragement of their parents, who also provide the youngsters with the necessary financial support in the form of pocket money.

7   The present research emphatically indicates that adult consumer behaviour is the direct antecedent of adolescent consumer behaviour which reflects that parents' adolescent-centredness forces them to accept the goods chosen by their adolescents in the household sector. Parents also seek adolescents' opinion even in purchasing products not directly related to the adolescents, such as cars, laptops, mobile phones because they have higher knowledge of brands, models and latest trends.

8   The study also lays stress on the fact that adolescents, no doubt, are emerging as major influencers in household buying decisions but still the final decision regarding the purchase of a product is in the hands of parents. Parents though have the final say while deciding to buy a product yet they always keep in mind the recommendations made by their adolescents regarding the purchase of that product.

5.4 Suggestions for Future Research

The primary aim of this research was to study the role of adolescents in buying decision making in Indian urban families. The work was aimed at analysing adolescents' role from parents' and adolescents' point of view. Based on the research carried and conclusions drawn, the following are the recommendations for future research.

The study has highlighted some important conclusions which emphasize the increasing role of adolescents in household buying decisions. The analysis also sets the stage for the following recommendations:

1   The first and the foremost job of the market researcher is to identify the role of each member of the household in the buying process and also the influence of each individual on the final decisions. The right purchase agent as well as user has to be identified in the light of the role of each constituent of the household.

2   The target group, the adolescents, should be motivated by their parents so that they should be free to express themselves and give their suggestions freely in the decision making process.

3   Marketers should make effective strategies by targeting not an individual member but each member of the household because each member of the household influences the decision making process in the purchase of different products, especially in the case of costly household products.

4   Adolescents should make the buying decisions consciously. Sometimes they make some wrong decisions because of their immaturity and promptness while buying products.

5   Adolescents should not be easily tempted towards the look and style of the product; rather they should see the products' use and durability.

6   It has been observed that adolescents act as purchasing agents and are delegated the task of purchasing products which they do not consume. Products for which adolescents act as purchasing agents should be identified by marketers which will help them to understand the features that are preferred by these purchasers and help in sending direct appropriate messages towards them.

7   At present, in India, there is a great shift in family structure. The joint family system is disappearing and more and more nuclear families, with or without working wives, are emerging; hence these shifts are to be gauged in the light of the changes occurring in the family types.

8   The complexity of the factors typical to the Indian marketing environment such as the prevalence of a joint nuclear family system, gifts of durables, large rural markets, means that studies need to be designed

more systematically to capture the effects of all the variables important in the Indian family context.

5.5 Concluding Remarks

To summarize, this research makes a significant contribution in the direction of role of adolescents in buying decision making. However, this study also helps to overcome the limitations that were encountered with the most methodological sound techniques. This study will encourage other researchers to engage into more research regarding adolescents and children with regard to common advantages and benefits.

Appendix

PART A: ADOLESCENTS

Name of the Adolescent	
Education	School / College
Gender	Male / Female
Age (in completed years)	10 11 12 13 14 15 16 17 18 19
Father's Occupation	Business / Service
Father's Qualification	Matric / Graduate / Post-Graduate
Mother's Qualification	Matric / Graduate / Post-Graduate
Mother's Occupation	Service / Housewife
Family's Annual Income	Up to 2 Lakhs / 2–5 Lakhs / 5–10 Lakhs / Above 10 Lakhs
Location	Punjab / Chandigarh / Haryana / N.A.
City	

	Item	Strongly Disagree (1)	Disagree (2)	Indifferent (3)	Agree (4)	Strongly Agree (5)
1	Father has a right to accept or reject any purchase decision at any time	1	2	3	4	5
2	Parents can easily impose their decision on their adolescents	1	2	3	4	5
3	Family member has his/her ideas relating to the products to be purchased	1	2	3	4	5
4	Parents feel that you are the younger generation and hence more aware to take your own decisions	1	2	3	4	5
5	Parents generally allow you to buy daily need products of your choice	1	2	3	4	5
6	Parents appreciate the things purchased by you	1	2	3	4	5
7	Parents feel dissatisfied regarding modified use of products after buying it	1	2	3	4	5
8	Since you are an important member of the family, you have the right to initiate and influence and also to decide sometimes regarding the purchase decision	1	2	3	4	5
9	Family members are egoistic about their self-concept in purchase matters	1	2	3	4	5
10	Educated members play an effective role in the decision making process	1	2	3	4	5
11	Change in income causes change in buying behaviour	1	2	3	4	5
12	Major part of the family income is spent by the adolescents	1	2	3	4	5
13	You give your consent in buying the costly products in the family	1	2	3	4	5
14	Are you the initiator/problem recognizer and hence the first person to demand the product	1	2	3	4	5
15	Switch from one brand to another for adventure	1	2	3	4	5

Item		Strongly Disagree (1)	Disagree (2)	Indifferent (3)	Agree (4)	Strongly Agree (5)
16	Advertisements have comparatively more impact on the minds of the adolescents	1	2	3	4	5
17	Promotional schemes like advertisements always lure you to buy the products	1	2	3	4	5
18	Rapid growth of market for adolescents' products is important	1	2	3	4	5

The following source of information influences purchasing Personal Consumable Items like _Gum, Candies, Chocolates, Ice Cream, Cold Drinks_

1	TV advertisements	1	2	3	4	5
2	Friends	1	2	3	4	5
3	Internet	1	2	3	4	5
4	Visit to store	1	2	3	4	5
5	Parents	1	2	3	4	5

The following source of information influences purchasing Personal Durable Items like _Shoes, Clothes, Video Games, School Stationery, Computer Games_

1	TV advertisements	1	2	3	4	5
2	Friends	1	2	3	4	5
3	Internet	1	2	3	4	5
4	Visit to store	1	2	3	4	5
5	Parents	1	2	3	4	5

The following source of information influences purchasing Family Toiletries Items like _Toothpaste, Soap, Shampoo, Cosmetics, Deodorant, Laundry Soap_

1	TV advertisements	1	2	3	4	5
2	Friends	1	2	3	4	5
3	Internet	1	2	3	4	5
4	Visit to store	1	2	3	4	5
5	Parents	1	2	3	4	5

The following source of information influences purchasing Family Electronics Items like *TV, Refrigerator, Telephone, Computer, DVD*

1	TV advertisements	1	2	3	4	5
2	Friends	1	2	3	4	5
3	Internet	1	2	3	4	5
4	Visit to store	1	2	3	4	5
5	Parents	1	2	3	4	5

The following source of information influences purchasing Family Automobile Items like *Car, Scooter, Motorcycle, Bicycle*

1	TV advertisements	1	2	3	4	5
2	Friends	1	2	3	4	5
3	Internet	1	2	3	4	5
4	Visit to store	1	2	3	4	5
5	Parents	1	2	3	4	5

The following source of information influences purchasing Other Product or Activities like *Movie Visit, Restaurant, Vacation*

1	TV advertisements	1	2	3	4	5
2	Friends	1	2	3	4	5
3	Internet	1	2	3	4	5
4	Visit to store	1	2	3	4	5
5	Parents	1	2	3	4	5

You influence decisions when buying personal consumable items

1	Gum, candies, chocolates	1	2	3	4	5
2	Ice creams	1	2	3	4	5
3	Soft drinks/cold drink	1	2	3	4	5
4	Health drinks	1	2	3	4	5
5	Fast foods (noodles, pasta)	1	2	3	4	5

Item	Strongly Disagree (1)	Disagree (2)	Indifferent (3)	Agree (4)	Strongly Agree (5)
You have an influence when buying durable items					
1 Shoes and footwear	1	2	3	4	5
2 Adolescents' clothes	1	2	3	4	5
3 School bags	1	2	3	4	5
4 Toys and video games (PC2/PC3)	1	2	3	4	5
5 Stationery items like pencils, pens	1	2	3	4	5
6 Magazine and comics	1	2	3	4	5
You influence buying the following products					
1 Go to movie	1	2	3	4	5
2 Restaurant	1	2	3	4	5
3 Family vacations	1	2	3	4	5
4 Visiting malls and supermarkets	1	2	3	4	5
Following source is important for *Entertainment*					
1 Magazine	1	2	3	4	5
2 Newspaper	1	2	3	4	5
3 Internet	1	2	3	4	5
4 TV	1	2	3	4	5
5 Radio	1	2	3	4	5
Following source is important for *Homework*					
1 Magazine	1	2	3	4	5
2 Newspaper	1	2	3	4	5
3 Internet	1	2	3	4	5
4 TV	1	2	3	4	5
5 Radio	1	2	3	4	5

Following source is important for _Sports related information_

1	Magazine	1	2	3	4	5
2	Newspaper	1	2	3	4	5
3	Internet	1	2	3	4	5
4	TV	1	2	3	4	5
5	Radio	1	2	3	4	5

Following source is important for _Cartoon_

1	Magazine	1	2	3	4	5
2	Newspaper	1	2	3	4	5
3	Internet	1	2	3	4	5
4	TV	1	2	3	4	5
5	Radio	1	2	3	4	5

You give importance to different kinds of appeals and demonstrations present in TV advertisements

1	Emotional appeal depicting social status like presence of celebrity in the advertisements	1	2	3	4	5
2	Emotional appeal depicting catchy phrases and words in form of jingles and slogans	1	2	3	4	5
3	Emotional appeal depicting use of adventure/action and thrilling scene	1	2	3	4	5
4	Emotional appeal depicting presence of striking scenes of nature scenes (mountains, flowing streams, etc.)	1	2	3	4	5

You behave in the following manner to get the advertised product from your parents

1	I make a very polite request to them	1	2	3	4	5
2	I keep on asking or saying please, please unless I get it	1	2	3	4	5
3	I make a direct request without explaining them any reason	1	2	3	4	5
4	I make money deals or labour deals in exchange for my purchases	1	2	3	4	5
5	I say that everyone has it like all my friends uses it	1	2	3	4	5

Item	Strongly Disagree (1)	Disagree (2)	Indifferent (3)	Agree (4)	Strongly Agree (5)
6 I do good deeds like cleaning the room	1	2	3	4	5
7 Acting affectionate like hugging them or saying how nice they look or showing too much love	1	2	3	4	5
8 I get mad and slam door or display anger verbally or non-verbally	1	2	3	4	5
9 I try to influence them through some people like aunts, grand-parents who can convince them	1	2	3	4	5
10 I act sad and go to my room and cry	1	2	3	4	5
Please tick whether you agree or disagree to the following statements					
1 TV advertisements are valuable source of information to me	1	2	3	4	5
2 I find TV advertisements quite amusing and entertaining	1	2	3	4	5
3 Sometimes I find TV advertisements are more enjoyable as compared to other media content	1	2	3	4	5
4 I would like to buy the brands advertised on TV	1	2	3	4	5
5 TV advertisements informs me about latest fashion trends	1	2	3	4	5
6 I like catchy punch lines in TV advertisements	1	2	3	4	5
7 I often ask my parents to buy what I saw in commercials	1	2	3	4	5
8 TV advertisements persuade me to like the product	1	2	3	4	5

PART B: PARENTS

	Item	Strongly Disagree (1)	Disagree (2)	Indifferent (3)	Agree (4)	Strongly Agree (5)
1	Adolescents want liberty of their expressions	1	2	3	4	5
2	Advertisement and media influence buying decision making	1	2	3	4	5
3	Purchase decision in a family is taken as one entity	1	2	3	4	5
4	You agree to the consent of your adolescents while buying a household product	1	2	3	4	5
5	In your family most of routine decisions are initiated by adolescents	1	2	3	4	5
6	Mother and adolescents are able to finance some of the purchase decisions rejected by the father	1	2	3	4	5
7	Adolescents oblige the financial conditions of the family	1	2	3	4	5
8	The actual buyers of the product are as much aware as the adolescents	1	2	3	4	5
9	Adolescents do not care for their needs and desires	1	2	3	4	5
10	Increasing use of TV and cinema affects the decision making role of the adolescents	1	2	3	4	5
11	When personal consumption is individual, the other family members take part in the decision	1	2	3	4	5
12	Adolescents have quick buying decisions	1	2	3	4	5
13	Adolescents are highly brand conscious	1	2	3	4	5
14	Adolescents are highly affected by physical attributes of a product	1	2	3	4	5
15	The cultural shift has brought about a change in the decision making process	1	2	3	4	5
16	The household income plays role in the decision making process for a purchase made for the adolescents	1	2	3	4	5

Item	Strongly Disagree (1)	Disagree (2)	Indifferent (3)	Agree (4)	Strongly Agree (5)
17 Adolescents are early adopters and make decisions in hurry	1	2	3	4	5
18 Adolescents play the role of mediator in any type of conflict in the decisions of the parents	1	2	3	4	5
19 You rely upon the information provided by your adolescents as you feel they are more updated because of media	1	2	3	4	5
20 Adolescents help in providing a final effect to the purchase decisions	1	2	3	4	5
21 Adolescents try to acquire appropriate knowledge about the product before they create an influence for change	1	2	3	4	5
22 Role models are important in adolescents' buying decisions	1	2	3	4	5
The following activities influence adolescents' buying behaviour					
1 Watching TV	1	2	3	4	5
2 Using the internet	1	2	3	4	5
3 Reading newspaper/magazines	1	2	3	4	5
4 Listening to the radio/FM	1	2	3	4	5
5 Online shopping	1	2	3	4	5
While making a buying decision you pay attention towards the following advertising media					
1 TV commercials	1	2	3	4	5
2 Newspaper advertisement	1	2	3	4	5
3 Advertisements on vehicles	1	2	3	4	5
4 Magazine advertisement	1	2	3	4	5
5 Billboard advertisement	1	2	3	4	5
6 Radio advertisement	1	2	3	4	5
7 Browser advertisement	1	2	3	4	5

Adolescents have influence while buying family toiletries

1	Toothpaste/brush	1	2	3	4	5
2	Soap bathing/face wash	1	2	3	4	5
3	Shampoo	1	2	3	4	5
4	Deodorant/perfumes	1	2	3	4	5
5	Household cleaning products	1	2	3	4	5
6	Cosmetics	1	2	3	4	5

Adolescents have influence while buying family electronics

1	TV	1	2	3	4	5
2	Refrigerator	1	2	3	4	5
3	Telephones, mobile phones	1	2	3	4	5
4	Video player, DVD	1	2	3	4	5
5	Computer	1	2	3	4	5

Adolescents have influence while buying family automobiles

1	Motorcycle	1	2	3	4	5
2	Car	1	2	3	4	5
3	Scooter	1	2	3	4	5
4	Bicycle	1	2	3	4	5

When your adolescent demands a product, you behave in the following manner

1	I ask my adolescent's opinion about product	1	2	3	4	5
2	I set price and products boundaries	1	2	3	4	5
3	I tell my adolescent the economic implication of the product	1	2	3	4	5
4	I compromise on purchase options with my adolescent	1	2	3	4	5
5	I make money deals or labour deals in exchange for his or her purchases	1	2	3	4	5
6	I tell him or her to make the purchase in reward for good behaviour	1	2	3	4	5
7	I give simple yes/no answer	1	2	3	4	5

Item	Strongly Disagree (1)	Disagree (2)	Indifferent (3)	Agree (4)	Strongly Agree (5)
8 Ignore the request	1	2	3	4	5
9 Postpone purchase	1	2	3	4	5
10 Can't afford	1	2	3	4	5

Following source is important for *Product related information search*

Item	Strongly Disagree (1)	Disagree (2)	Indifferent (3)	Agree (4)	Strongly Agree (5)
1 Magazine	1	2	3	4	5
2 Newspaper	1	2	3	4	5
3 Internet	1	2	3	4	5
4 TV	1	2	3	4	5
5 Radio	1	2	3	4	5

Following source is important for *Leisure time*

Item	Strongly Disagree (1)	Disagree (2)	Indifferent (3)	Agree (4)	Strongly Agree (5)
1 Magazine	1	2	3	4	5
2 Newspaper	1	2	3	4	5
3 Internet	1	2	3	4	5
4 TV	1	2	3	4	5
5 Radio	1	2	3	4	5

Following source is important for *Information of current events*

Item	Strongly Disagree (1)	Disagree (2)	Indifferent (3)	Agree (4)	Strongly Agree (5)
1 Magazine	1	2	3	4	5
2 Newspaper	1	2	3	4	5
3 Internet	1	2	3	4	5
4 TV	1	2	3	4	5
5 Radio	1	2	3	4	5

You give importance to different kinds of appeals and demonstrations present in TV advertisements

1	Emotional appeal for creation of mood and emotions	1	2	3	4	5
2	Rational appeal depicting taste, health and nutrients claims in the product	1	2	3	4	5
3	Rational appeal depicting economy and savings in the purchase of product	1	2	3	4	5

Whether you agree or disagree to the following statements

1	I get irritated when TV advertisements are there mid programme	1	2	3	4	5
2	TV advertisements present true features of the product advertised	1	2	3	4	5
3	I don't believe everything TV commercials tell me	1	2	3	4	5
4	TV advertisements provide information about new products launched in the market	1	2	3	4	5
5	I think TV advertisements are misleading as they only show good things about the product advertised	1	2	3	4	5
6	When TV commercials are there I change the channel	1	2	3	4	5

PART C: PRIORITY QUESTIONNAIRE

Please indicate the relative importance of following advertising media

TV commercials	1 3 5 7 9	Newspaper advertisement
TV commercials	1 3 5 7 9	Advertisements on vehicles
TV commercials	1 3 5 7 9	Magazine advertisement
TV commercials	1 3 5 7 9	Billboard advertisement
TV commercials	1 3 5 7 9	Radio advertisement
TV commercials	1 3 5 7 9	Browser advertisement
Newspaper advertisement	1 3 5 7 9	Advertisements on vehicles
Newspaper advertisement	1 3 5 7 9	Magazine advertisement
Newspaper advertisement	1 3 5 7 9	Billboard advertisement
Newspaper advertisement	1 3 5 7 9	Radio advertisement
Newspaper advertisement	1 3 5 7 9	Browser advertisement
Advertisements on vehicles	1 3 5 7 9	Magazine advertisement
Advertisements on vehicles	1 3 5 7 9	Billboard advertisement
Advertisements on vehicles	1 3 5 7 9	Radio advertisement
Advertisements on vehicles	1 3 5 7 9	Browser advertisement
Magazine advertisement	1 3 5 7 9	Billboard advertisement
Magazine advertisement	1 3 5 7 9	Radio advertisement
Magazine advertisement	1 3 5 7 9	Browser advertisement
Billboard advertisement	1 3 5 7 9	Radio advertisement
Billboard advertisement	1 3 5 7 9	Browser advertisement
Radio advertisement	1 3 5 7 9	Browser advertisement

Please indicate the relative importance of activities for decision making

Entertainment	1 3 5 7 9	Homework
Entertainment	1 3 5 7 9	Listening music
Entertainment	1 3 5 7 9	Product related information search
Entertainment	1 3 5 7 9	Sports related information
Entertainment	1 3 5 7 9	Leisure time
Entertainment	1 3 5 7 9	Cartoon
Entertainment	1 3 5 7 9	Information of current events
Homework	1 3 5 7 9	Listening music
Homework	1 3 5 7 9	Product related information search
Homework	1 3 5 7 9	Sports related information
Homework	1 3 5 7 9	Leisure time
Homework	1 3 5 7 9	Cartoon
Homework	1 3 5 7 9	Information of current events
Listening to music	1 3 5 7 9	Product related information search
Listening to music	1 3 5 7 9	Sports related information
Listening to music	1 3 5 7 9	Leisure time
Listening to music	1 3 5 7 9	Cartoon
Listening to music	1 3 5 7 9	Information of current events

Product related information search	1 3 5 7 9	Sports related information
Product related information search	1 3 5 7 9	Leisure time
Product related information search	1 3 5 7 9	Cartoon
Product related information search	1 3 5 7 9	Information of current events
Sports related information	1 3 5 7 9	Leisure time
Sports related information	1 3 5 7 9	Cartoon
Sports related information	1 3 5 7 9	Information of current events
Leisure time	1 3 5 7 9	Cartoon
Leisure time	1 3 5 7 9	Information of current events
Cartoon	1 3 5 7 9	Information of current events

References

Achenreiner, G. B. (1997) "Materialistic values and susceptibility to influence in children", *Advances in Consumer Research*, *24*, 82–88.

Adib, H. and El-Bassiouny, N. (2012) "Materialism in young consumers: An investigation of family communication patterns and parental mediation practices in Egypt", *Journal of Islamic Marketing*, *3*(3), 255–282.

Ahluwalia, A. K. and Sanan, P. (2016) "Consumer awareness and consumer activism among adolescents: A socialization perspective", *IUP Journal of Marketing Management, 15*(1), 49–73.

Ahmad, M., Sidin, S. M. and Omar, N. A. (2011) "A preliminary investigation of adolescents' perception of the role of internet in parent consumer socialization", *IUP Journal of Marketing Management*, *10*(3), 7–16.

Ahuja, R. D. and Stinson. K. M. (1993) "Female-headed single parent families: An exploratory study of children's influence in family decision making", *Advances in Consumer Research*, *20*, 469–474.

Alsmadi, S., & Khizindar, T. (2015) "Consumers' perceptions of consumer rights in Jordan", *International Journal of Commerce and Management*, *25*(4), 512–530.

Andersen, L. P., Tufte, B., Rasmussen, J. and Chan, K. (2007) "Tweens and new media in Denmark and Hong Kong", *Journal of Consumer Marketing*, *24*(6), 340–350.

Aoud, H. N. and Neeley, M. S. (2008) "Teenager–peer interaction and its contribution to a family purchase decision: The mediating role of enduring product involvement", *International Journal of Consumer Studies*, *32*, 242–252.

Assael, H. (1992) *Consumer behavior and marketing action* (4th edn). Boston, MA: PWs-KENT Publishing Co.

Atkin, C. K. (1978) "Observation of parent–child interaction in supermarket decision-making", *Journal of Marketing*, *42*(4), 41–45.

Austin, E. W., Bolls, P., Fujioka, Y. and Engelbertson, J. (1999) "How and why parents take on the tube", *Journal of Broadcasting & Electronic Media*, *43*(2), 175–192.

Baker, S. M. and Gentry, J. W. (1996) "Kids as collectors: A phenomenological study of first and fifth graders", *Advances in Consumer Research*, *23*(1), 132–137.

Barber, N. A. (2013) "Investigating the potential influence of the internet as a new socialization agent in context with other traditional socialization agents", *Journal of Marketing Theory and Practice, 21*(2), 179–194.

Barling, J. and Fullagar, C. (1983) "Children's attitudes to television advertisements: A factorial perspective", *Journal of Psychology, 113*, 25–30.

Beatty, S. E. and Talpade, S. (1994) "Adolescent influence in family decision making: A replication with extension", *Journal of Consumer Research, 21*(2), 332–341.

Beaudoin, P. and Lachance, M. J. (2006) "Determinants of adolescents' brand sensitivity to clothing", *Family and Consumer Sciences Research Journal, 34*(4), 312–331.

Belch, G. E., Belch, M. and Ceresino, G. (1985) "Parental and teenage influences in family decision-making", *Journal of Business Research, 13*, 163–176.

Belch, M. A., Krentler, K. A. and Willis-Flurry, L. A. (2005) "Teen internet mavens: Influence in family decision making", *Journal of Business Research, 58*(5), 569–575.

Belk, R. W. (1985) "Materialism: Trait aspects of living in the material world", *Journal of Consumer Research, 12*(3), 265–280.

Bergadaà, M. (2007) "Children and business: Pluralistic ethics of marketers", *Society and Business Review, 2*(1), 53–73.

Beyda, T. T. (2010) "Who teaches them to consume: A study of Brazilian youngsters", *International Journal of Consumer Studies, 34*(3), 298–305.

Bhupta, M. and Pai, A. (2007) "No kidding", *India Today*, 25 June, 50–57.

Bian, Q. and Forsythe, S. (2012) "Purchase intention for luxury brands: A cross cultural comparison", *Journal of Business Research, 65*(10), 1443–1451.

Boon, C. C. T., Md Sidin, S., Nor, M. and Izzudin, M. (2013) "Exploring influences of consumer socialization agents on branded apparel purchase among urban Malaysian tweens", *Pertanika Journal of Social Sciences & Humanities, 21*(1), 1–16.

Boyland, E. J., Harrold, J. A., Kirkham, T. C. and Halford, J. C. G. (2011) "Persuasive techniques used in television advertisements to market foods to UK children", *Appetite, 58*(2), 658–664.

Brim, O. G., Jr. (1966) "Socialization through the life cycle". In O. G. Brim, Jr. and S. Wheeler (eds), *Socialization after childhood: Two essays* (pp. 1–49). New York: John Wiley.

Brucks, M., Zeithaml, V. A. and Naylor, G. (2000) "Price and brand name as indicators of quality dimensions for consumer durables", *Journal of the Academy of Marketing Science, 28*(3), 359–374.

Buijzen, M. and Valkenburg, M. P. (2002) "The unintended effects of television advertising", *Journal of Communication Research, 30*(5), 483–503.

Burgess, S. M. and Steenkamp, J. B. E. (2006) "Marketing renaissance: How research in emerging markets advances marketing science and practice", *International Journal of Research in Marketing, 23*(4), 337–356.

Cakarnis, J. and D'Alessandro, S. P. (2015) "Does knowing overcome wanting? The impact of consumer knowledge and materialism upon credit card selection with young consumers", *Young Consumers, 16*(1), 50–70.

Carlson, L. and Grossbart, S. (1988) "Parental style and consumer socialization of children", *Journal of Consumer Research*, *15*(1), 77–94.

Cartwright, N. (1999) *The dappled world: A study of the boundaries of science.* Cambridge: Cambridge University Press.

Census of India (2011) "Provisional population totals paper 1", Office of the Registrar General & Census Commissioner, India.

Chan, K. (2008) "Chinese children's perceptions of advertising and brands: An urban rural comparison", *Journal of Consumer Marketing*, *25*(2), 74–84.

Chan, K. (2013) "Development of materialistic values among children and adolescents", *Young Consumers, 14*(3), 244–257.

Chan, K. and Fang, W. (2007) "Use of the internet and traditional media among young people", *Young Consumer*, *8*(4), 244–256.

Chan, K. and McNeal, J. U. (2002) "Parental concern about television viewing and children's advertising in China". *International Journal for Public Opinion Research, 15*(2), 150–166.

Chan, K. and McNeal, J. U. (2006) "Children's perception of television advertising in urban China", *International Journal of Advertising and Marketing to Children, 3*(3), 69–79.

Chaplin, L. N. and John, D. R. (2007) "Growing up in a material world: Age differences in materialism in children and adolescents", *Journal of Consumer Research, 34*(4), 480–493.

Chaplin, L. N. and John, D. R. (2010) "Interpersonal influences on adolescent materialism: A new look at the role of parents and peers", *Journal of Consumer Psychology, 20*(2), 176–184.

Chaplin, L. N., Hill, R. P. and John, D. R. (2014) "Poverty and materialism: A look at impoverished versus affluent children", *Journal of Public Policy & Marketing, 33*(1), 78–92.

Chaudhary, M. and Gupta, A. (2014) "Children's consumer socialisation agents in India", *International Journal of Business Innovation and Research*, *8*(1), 76–93.

Cheng C. (1993) "Little emperors make big consumers", *China Today*, *42*, 47–49.

Chia, S. C. (2010) "How social influence mediates media effects on adolescents' materialism", *Communication Research, 37*(3), 400–419.

Churchill, G. A. and Moschis, G. P. (1979) "Television and interpersonal influences on adolescent consumer learning", *Journal of Consumer Research, 6*(1), 23–35.

Clarke, J. (2002) "The internet according to kids", *Journal of Advertising and Marketing to Children*, 45–52.

Clark, P. W., Martin, C. A. and Bush, A. J. (2001) "The effect of role model influence on adolescents' materialism and marketplace knowledge", *Journal of Marketing Theory and Practice, 9*(4), 27–36.

Cude, B., Lawrence, F., Lyons, A., Metzger, K., LeJeune, E., Marks, L. and Machtmes, K. (2006) "College students and financial literacy: What they know and what we need to learn", *Proceedings of the Eastern Family Economics and Resource Management Association*, 102–109.

D'Alessio, M., Laghi, F. and Baiocco, R. (2009) "Attitudes toward TV advertising: A measure for children", *Journal of Applied Developmental Psychology, 30*(4), 409–418.

Davey, G. (2008) "Children's television, radio, internet, and computer usage in a city and a village of China", *Visual Anthropology, 21*, 160–165.

Davie, R., Panting, C. and Charlton, T. (2004) "Mobile phone ownership and usage among pre-adolescents", *Telematics and Informatics, 21*(4), 359–373.

Davis, H. L. (1976) "Decision making within the household", *Journal of Consumer Research, 2*, 241–260.

Dens, N., De Pelsmacker, P. and Eagle, L. (2007) "Parental attitudes towards advertising to children and restrictive mediation of children's television viewing in Belgium", *Young Consumer, 8*(1), 7–18.

Derbaix, C. and Pecheux, C. (2003) "A new scale to assess children's attitude towards TV advertising", *Journal of Advertising Research, 43*(4), 390–399.

Devís Devís, J., Peiró-Velert, C., Beltran-Carrillo, V. J. and Tomás, J. M. (2009) "Screen media time usage of 12–16 year-old Spanish school adolescents: Effects of personal and socioeconomic factors, season and type of day", *Journal of Adolescence, 32*, 213–231.

Dhobal, S. (1999) "NUFgen marketing or selling to the new urban family", *Business Today, 22*, 66–81.

Dix, S., Phau, I. and Pougnet, S. (2010) " 'Bend it like Beckham': The influence of sports celebrities on young adult consumers", *Young Consumers, 11*(1), 36–46.

Dotson, M. J. and Hyatt, E. M. (2005) "Major influence factors in children's consumer socialization", *Journal of Consumer Marketing, 22*(1), 35–42.

Drentea, P. and Lavrakas, P. J. (2000) "Over the limit: The association among health, race and debt", *Social Science & Medicine, 50*(4), 517–529.

Dursun, Y. (1993) "Young's acquisitions of the consumer role". PhD Thesis. Institute of Social Science, Erciyes University, Kayseri.

Ekstrom, K. M., Tansuhaj, P. S. and Foxman, E. R. (1987) "Children's influence in family decisions and consumer socialization: A reciprocal view", *Advances in Consumer Research, 14*, 283–287.

El-Adly, M. I. (2010) "The impact of advertising attitudes on the intensity of TV ads avoiding behavior", *International Journal of Business and Social Science, 1*(1): 1–18.

Estrela, R. C., Costa Pereira, F. and Bruno Ventura, J. (2014) "Children's socialization in consumption: The role of marketing", *EuroMed Journal of Business, 9*(3), 222–251.

Fiates, G. M. R., De Mello Amboni, R. D. and Teixeira, E. (2008) "Consumer behaviour of Brazilian primary school students: Findings from focus group interviews", *International Journal of Consumer Studies, 32*, 157–162.

Field, A. (2000) *Discovering statistics using SPSS for Windows*. London, Thousand Oaks, New Delhi: Sage Publications.

Flouri, E. (2004) "Exploring the relationship between mothers' and fathers' parenting practices and children's materialist values", *Journal of Economic Psychology, 25*(6), 743–752.

Foxman, E., Tansuhaj, P. and Ekstrom, K. M. (1989a). "Adolescents' influence in family purchase decisions: A socialization perspective", *Journal of Business Research, 18*, 159–172.

Foxman, E., Tansuhaj, P. and Ekstrom, K. (1989b) "Family members' perceptions of adolescents' influence in family decision marking. *Journal of Consumer Research*, *15*, 482–491.

Fu, X., Kou, Y. and Yang, Y. (2015) "Materialistic values among Chinese adolescents: Effects of parental rejection and self-esteem", *Child & Youth Care Forum*, *44*(1), 43–57.

Galst, J. and White, M. (1976) "The unhealthy persuader: The reinforcing value of television and children's purchase-influencing attempts at the supermarket", *Child Development*, *47*(4), 1089–1096.

Ganapatthy, V. (2009) "Power of humor in advertising", *Advertising Express*, 21–33.

Ghani, N. H. A. and Zain, O. M. (2004) "Malaysian children's attitudes towards television advertising", *Journal of Advertising and Marketing to Children*, April –June, 41–51.

Goldsmith, R. E., Flynn, L. R. and Kim, D. (2010) "Status consumption and price sensitivity", *Journal of Marketing Theory and Practice*, *18*(4), 323–338.

Gudmunson, C. G. and Beutler, I. F. (2012) "Relation of parental caring to conspicuous consumption attitudes in adolescents", *Journal of Family and Economic Issues*, *33*(4), 389–399.

Habing, B. (2003). "Exploratory factor analysis" (www.stat.sc.edu/~habing/courses/530EFA.pdf).

Halan, D. (2002) "Why kids mean business", *Indian Management*, *41*(12), 46–49.

Haq, M. R. and Rahman, S. H. (2015) "Role of reality TV as a consumer-socialization agent of teenagers in a developing country", *International Journal of Emerging Markets*, *10*(3), 598–618.

Hart, C. (1998) *Doing a literature review: Releasing the social science research imagination*. London: Sage Publications.

Haverilla, M. (2012) "What do we want specifically from the cell phone? An age related study", *Telematics and Informatics*, *29*, 110–122.

Hawkins, C. H. (1977) "A study of the use of consumer education concepts by high school graduates", *Journal of Consumer Affairs*, *11*(1), 122–127.

Hawkins, D. I. and Coney, K. A. (1974) "Peer group influence on children's product preferences", *Journal of the Academy of Marketing Science*, *2*(2), 322–331.

Hayta, A. B. (2008) "Socialization of the child as a consumer", *Family and Consumer Sciences Research Journal*, *37*(2), 167–184.

Hundal, B. S. (2001) "Consumer behaviour in rural market: A study of durables". Unpublished Doctoral Dissertation, Guru Nanak Dev University, Amritsar.

Hurlock, E. B. (1968) "The adolescent reformer", *Adolescence*, *3*(11), 273–285.

Hwang, C. L. and Yoon, K. (1981) *Multiple attribute decision making: Methods and applications*. New York: Springer-Verlag.

Ishak, S. and Zabil, N. F. M. (2012) "Impact of consumer awareness and knowledge to consumer effective behavior", *Asian Social Science*, *8*(13), 108–114.

Jensen, J. M. (1995) "Children's purchase requests and parental responses: Results from an exploratory study in Denmark", *European Advances in Consumer Research*, *2*, 54–60.

John, D. R. (1999) "Consumer socialization of children: A retrospective look at twenty-five years of research", *Journal of Consumer Research, 26*(3), 183–213.

Johnson, M. (1995) "The impact of product and situational factors on the choice of conflict resolution strategies by children in family purchase decision making", *European Advances in Consumer Research, 2*, 61–68.

Johnsson-Smaragdi, U., Leen d'Haenens, F. F. and Hasebrink. U. (1998) "Patterns of old and new media use among young people in Flanders, Germany and Sweden", *European Journal of Communication, 12*(4), 479–501.

Jorgensen, B. L. and Savla, J. (2010) "Financial literacy of young adults: The importance of parental socialization", *Family Relations, 59*(4), 465–478.

Kapoor, N. and Verma, D. P. S. (2004) "Children's understanding of TV advertisements: Influence of age and parents", *Vision – The Journal of Business Perspective, 9*(1), 21–36.

Kapoor, S. (2001) "Family influence on purchase decision: A study with reference to consumer durables". Unpublished Doctoral Dissertation, University of Delhi.

Kaur, A. and Medury, Y. (2011) "Impact of the internet on teenagers' influence on family purchases", *Young Consumers, 12*(1), 27–38.

Kaur, P. and Singh, R. (2004) "Role structures in the buying decision process for durables", *Paradigm,* January–June.

Kaur, P. and Singh, R. (2006) "Children in family purchase decision making in India and the West: A", *Academy of Marketing Science Review, 8*, 1–30.

Kim, D. and Jang, S. S. (2014) "Motivational drivers for status consumption: A study of Generation Y consumers", *International Journal of Hospitality Management, 38*, 39–47.

Klein, N. (2000) *No logo: Taking aim at the brand bullies.* Toronto: Knopf Canada.

Kubey, R. and Larson, R. (1990) "The use and experience of the new video media among children and young adolescents", *Journal of Communication Research, 17*(1), 107–130.

Kunkel, D. (1992) "Children's television advertising in the multichannel environment", *Journal of Communication, 42*(3), 134–152.

La Ferle, C. and Chan, K. (2008) "Determinants for materialism among adolescents in Singapore", *Young Consumers, 9*(3), 201–214.

Lachance, M. J. and Legault, F. (2007) "College students' consumer competence: Identifying the socialization sources", *Journal of Research for Consumers, 13*, 1–5.

Lachance, M. J., Beaudoin, P. and Robitaille, J. (2003) "Adolescents' brand sensitivity in apparel: Influence of three socialization agents", *International Journal of Consumer Studies, 27*(1), 47–57.

Lachance, M. J., Legault, F. and Bujold, N. (2000) Family structure, parent–child communication, and adolescent participation in family consumer tasks and discussion. *Family and Consumer Sciences Research Journal, 29*(2), 125–152.

Langrehr, F. W. (1979) "Consumer education: Does it change students' competencies and attitudes?" *Journal of Consumer Affairs, 13*(1), 41–53.

Langrehr, F. W. and Barry, M. J. (1977) "The development and implementation of the concept of consumer education", *Journal of Consumer Affairs (Pre-1986), 11*(2), 63–80.

Larkin, E. (1977) "A factor analysis of college student attitudes toward advertising", *Journal of Advertising*, *1*, 42–46.

Lawlor, M. A. and Prothero, A. (2003) "Children's understanding of television advertising intent", *Journal of Marketing Management*, *19*, 411–431.

Lee, C. K. C. and Beatty, S. E. (2002) "Family structure and influence in family decision making", *Journal of Consumer Marketing*, *19*(1), 24–41.

Lee, C. K. C. and Collins, B. A. (1999). "Family decision making and coalition patterns", Department of Marketing, University of Auckland, New Zealand.

Lee, C. K. and Conroy, D. M. (2005) "Socialisation through consumption: Teenagers and the internet", *Australasian Marketing Journal (AMJ)*, *13*(1), 8–19.

Lee, C. K., Conroy, D. M. and Hii, C. (2003) "The internet: A consumer socialization agent for teenagers", *ANZMAC Conference Proceedings*, 1708–1715.

Leistritz, F. L., Ekstrom, B. L., Wanzek, J. K. and Vreugdenhil, H. G. (1987) "Selected socioeconomic characteristics of North Dakota community residents", *Agricultural Economics Reports 23217*, North Dakota State University, Department of Agribusiness and Applied Economics.

Levy, D. (1996) "The influence of family members on housing purchase decisions", *Journal of Property Investment and Finance*, *14*, 320–338.

Lindstrom, M. (2004) "The real decision makers" (www.brandchannel.com/brand_speak.asp?).

Lueg, J. E. and Ponder, N. (2006) "Understanding the socialisation process of teen consumers across shopping channels", *International Journal of Electronic Marketing and Retailing*, *1*(1), 83–97.

Lyons, A. C. and Hunt, J. (2003) "The credit practices and financial education needs of community college students", *Journal of Financial Counseling and Planning*, *14*(2), 63–74.

McCroskey, J. C. (2006) "Reliability and validity of the generalized attitude measure and generalized belief measure", *Communication Quarterly*, *54*(3), 265–274.

McDonald, G. W. (1980) "Family power: The assessment of a decade of theory and research, 1970–1979", *Journal of Marriage and the Family*, *42*(November), 841–854.

McLeod, J. M. (1974) "Commentaries on Ward, 'consumer socialization'", *Journal of Consumer Research*, *1*(September), 15–26.

McLeod, J. M., Fitzpatrick, M. A., Glynn, C. J. and Fallis, S. F. (1982) "Television and social relations: Family influences and consequences for interpersonal behavior", *Television and Behavior: Ten Years of Scientific Progress and Implications for the Eighties*, *2*, 272–286.

McNeal, J. U. (1979) "Children as consumers: A review", *Journal of the Academy of Marketing Science*, *7*(4), 346–359.

McNeal, J. U. (1992) *Kids as consumers: A handbook of marketing to children.* Oxford, UK: Lexington Books.

McNeal, J. (1999) *The kids market: Myths and realities.* New York: Paramount Publishing.

McNeal, J. and Hwa Yeh (1997) "Children as consumers of commercial and social products", cited in A. B. Hayta, "Socialization of the child as a consumer", *Family and Consumer Science Research Journal*, *34*(3), 167–184.

McNeal, J. U. and Ji, M. F. (1999) "Chinese children as consumers: An analysis of their new product information sources", *Journal of Consumer Marketing, 16*(4), 345–365.

Maheshwari, U. P. (2009) "Animation in advertising", *Advertising Express*, 14–18.

Mahima, S. T. and Khatri, P. (2008) "Relationship between parental over-indulgence and buying behaviour in the context of invasive marketing: A comparative study of two cultures", *Seoul Journal of Business, 14*(1), 31–53.

Makela, C. J. and Peters, S. (2004) "Consumer education: Creating consumer awareness among adolescents in Botswana", *International Journal of Consumer Studies, 28*(4), 379–387.

Mallalieu, L. and Palan, K. M. (2006) "How good a shopper am I? Conceptualizing teenage girls' perceived shopping competence", *Academy of Marketing Science Review, 5*, 1–14.

Mangleburg, T. F., Doney, P. M. and Bristol, T. (2004) "Shopping with friends and teens' susceptibility to peer influence", *Journal of Retailing, 80*(2), 101–116.

Manuel Sancho, F., Jose Miguel, M. and Aldás, J. (2011) "Factors influencing youth alcohol consumption intention: An approach from consumer socialization theory", *Journal of Social Marketing, 1*(3), 192–210.

Martin, A. and Oliva, J. C. (2001) "Teaching children about money: Applications of social learning and cognitive learning developmental theories", *Journal of Family and Consumer Sciences: From Research to Practice, 93*(2), 26–29.

Martin, C. A. and Turley, L. W. (2004) "Malls and consumption motivation: An exploratory examination of older Generation Y consumers", *International Journal of Retail & Distribution Management, 32*(10), 464–475.

Mayer, R. (1994) "Planning priorities for marketing to children", *Journal of Business Strategy*, (May/June), 12–15.

Mehrotra, S. and Torges, S. (1977) "Determinants of children's influence on mothers' buying behaviour", *Advances in Consumer Research, 4*, 56–60.

Mehta, S. C. and Keng, J. L. L. (1985) "Consumer socialization: An empirical investigation into Singapore adolescents", *SV-Historical Perspective in Consumer Research: National and International Perspectives*, 320–325.

Miller, J. H. and Busch, P. (1979) "Host selling vs. premium TV commercials: An experimental evaluation of their influence on children", *Journal of Marketing Research, 12*, 323–332.

Mizerski, R. (1995) "The relationship between cartoon trade character recognition and attitude toward product category in young children", *Journal of Marketing, 59*(4), 58–70.

Mangleburg, T. F., Grewal, D. and Bristol, T. (1999) "Family type, family authority relations, and adolescents' purchase influence", *Advances in Consumer Research, 26*, 379–384.

Mittal, M., Daga, A., Chhabra, G. and Lilani, J. (2010) "Parental perception of the impact of television advertisements on children's buying behavior", *IUP Journal of Marketing Management, IX*(1 & 2), 40–54.

Moore, D. S. and McCabe, G. P. (2006) *Introduction to the practice of statistics* (5th edn). New York: Freeman.

Moore, R. L. and Moschis, G. P. (1981) "The role of family communication in consumer learning", *Journal of Communication*, *31*(4), 42–51.

Moore, R. and Stephens, L. (1975) "Some communication and demographic determinants of adolescent consumer learning", *Journal of Consumer Research*, *2*(2), 80–92.

Moscardelli, D. and Liston-Heyes, C. (2005) "Consumer socialization in a wired world: The effects of internet use and parental communication on the development of skepticism to advertising", *Journal of Marketing Theory and Practice*, *13*(3), 62–75.

Moschis, G. P. (1976) "Shopping orientations and consumer uses of information", *Journal of Retailing*, *52*(2), 61.

Moschis, G. P. (1979) "Formal consumer education: An empirical assessment", *Advances in Consumer Research*, *6*(1), 456–59.

Moschis, G. (1985) "The role of family communication in consumer socialization of children and adolescents", *Journal of Consumer Research*, *11*(4), 898–913.

Moschis, G. P. and Churchill Jr, G. A. (1978) "Consumer socialization: A theoretical and empirical analysis", *Journal of Marketing Research*, *15*(4), 599–609.

Moschis, G. and Churchill, G. (1979) "An analysis of the adolescent consumer", *Journal of Marketing*, *43*(3), 40–48.

Moschis, G. P. and Moore, R. L. (1978) "An analysis of the acquisition of some consumer competencies among adolescents", *Journal of Consumer Affairs*, *12*(2), 277–291.

Moschis, G. P. and Moore, R. L. (1979) "Decision making among the young: A socialization perspective", *Journal of Consumer Research*, *6*(2), 101–112.

Moschis, G. and Moore, R. (1982) "A longitudinal study of television advertising effects", *Journal of Consumer Research*, *9*(3), 279–286.

Moschis, G. P., Moore, R. L. and Smith, R. B. (1984a) "The impact of family communication on adolescent consumer socialization", *Advances in Consumer Research*, *11*(1), 314–319.

Moschis, G. P., Moore, R. L. and Stanley, T. J. (1984b) "An exploratory study of brand loyalty development", *Advances in Consumer Research*, *11*(1), 412–417.

Moschis, G. P., Prahato, A. E. and Mitchell, L. G. (1986) "Family communication influences on the development of consumer behavior: Some additional findings", *Advances in Consumer Research*, *13*(1), 365–369.

Moschis, G., Sim Ong, F., Mathur, A., Yamashita, T. and Benmoyal-Bouzaglo, S. (2011) "Family and television influences on materialism: A cross-cultural life-course approach", *Journal of Asia Business Studies*, *5*(2), 124–144.

Mukherjee, N. (2006) "MS and master splurge", *The Week*, *3* September, 40–48.

Mukherji, J. (2006) "Maternal communication patterns, advertising attitudes and mediation behaviours in urban India", *Journal of Marketing Communications*, *11*(4), 247–262.

Nazık, H. and Nakılcıoğlu, K. (2002) "A research on the determination of the effect of the commercials on the families' consumption behaviors", *Standard Economic and Technique Magazine*, *40*(476), 80–87.

North, E. J. and Kotzé, T. (2001) "Parents and television advertisements as consumer socialisation agents for adolescents: An exploratory study", *Journal of*

Family Ecology and Consumer Sciences/Tydskrif vir Gesinsekologie en Verbruikerswetenskappe, *29*(1), 91–99.

Nunnaly, J. C. (1978) *Psychometric theory*. New York: McGraw-Hill.

Nusair, K., Jin Yoon, H., Naipaul, S. and Parsa, H. G. (2010) "Effect of price discount frames and levels on consumers' perceptions in low-end service industries", *International Journal of Contemporary Hospitality Management*, *22*(6), 814–835.

O'Cass, A. and McEwen, H. (2004) "Exploring consumer status and conspicuous consumption", *Journal of Consumer Behaviour*, *4*(1), 25–39.

O'Cass, A. and Siahtiri, V. (2013) "In search of status through brands from Western and Asian origins: Examining the changing face of fashion clothing consumption in Chinese young adults", *Journal of Retailing and Consumer Services*, *20*(6), 505–515.

O'Guinn, T. and Shrum, L. (1997) "The role of television in the construction of consumer reality", *Journal of Consumer Research*, *23*(4), 278–294.

Oates, C., Blades, M., Gunter, B. and Don, J. (2003) "Children's understanding of television advertising: A qualitative approach", *Journal of Marketing Communications*, *9*(2), 59–71.

Opree, S. J., Buijzen, M., van Reijmersdal, E. A. and Valkenburg, P. M. (2014) "Children's advertising exposure, advertised product desire, and materialism: A longitudinal study", *Communication Research*, *41*(5), 717–735.

Ozgen, O. (1995) "The living period approach towards socialization of consumer", *Standard Economic and Technique Magazine*, *41*(483), 425–40.

Ozmete, E. (2009) "Parent and adolescent interaction in television advertisements as consumer socialization agents", *Education*, *129*(3), 372–381.

Page, M. R. and Brewster, A. (2007) Frequency of promotional strategies and attention elements in children's food commercials during children's programming blocks on US broadcast networks", *Young Consumers*, *18*, 184–196.

Palan, K. M. and Wilkes, R. E. (1997) "Adolescent–parent interaction in family decision making", *Journal of Consumer Research*, *24*(2), 159–169.

Pandey, M. (2010) "Impact of celebrities' multiple product endorsements on buyer's attitude and purchase intentions", *Indian Journal of Marketing*, 3–12.

Parasuraman, A. (1991) "Perceived service quality as a customer-based performance measure: An empirical examination of organizational barriers using an extended service quality model", *Human Resource Management*, *30*(3), 335–364.

Petrovici, D. and Marinov, M. (2005) "Determinants and antecedents of general attitudes towards advertising", *European Journal of Marketing*, *41*, 3–4.

Pettigrew, S. and Roberts, M. (2006) "Mothers' attitudes towards toys as fast food premiums", *Young Consumers*, *3*, 60–67.

Phau, I. and Cheong, E. (2009) "How young adult consumers evaluate diffusion brands: Effects of brand loyalty and status consumption", *Journal of International Consumer Marketing*, *21*(2), 109–123.

Pollay, R. W. and Mittal, B. (1993) "Here's the beef: Factors, determinants, and segments in consumer criticism of advertising", *Journal of Marketing*, *57*, 99–114.

Prabhi, G. (2009) "Advertising: A buzzword for brand recall", *Advertising Express*, 17–21.

Qualls, W. J. (1982) "Sex roles, its impact on family decision making", *Advances in Consumer Research*, 267–270.

Raskin, R. N. and Hall, C. S. (1979) "A narcissistic personality inventory", *Psychological Reports*, 45(2), 590–590.

Raskin, R. and Terry, H. (1988) "A principal-components analysis of the Narcissistic Personality Inventory and further evidence of its construct validity", *Journal of Personality and Social Psychology*, *54*, 890–902.

Richins, M. L. and Dawson, S. (1992) "A consumer values orientation for materialism and its measurement: Scale development and validation", *Journal of Consumer Research*, *19*(3), 303–316.

Riesman, D. and Roseborough, H. (1955) "Careers and consumer behavior", *Consumer Behavior*, 2, 1–18.

Roberts, D. F. (2000) "Media and youth: Access, exposure, and privatization", *Journal of Adolescent Health*, 27, 8–14.

Roberts, J. A., Manolis, C. and John, F. (2003) "Family structure, materialism, and compulsive buying: A reinquiry and extension", *Academy of Marketing Science Journal*, *31*(3), 300–312.

Roberts, J. A., Manolis, C. and John, F. (2006) "Adolescent autonomy and the impact of family structure on materialism and compulsive buying", *Journal of Marketing Theory and Practice*, *14*(4), 301–314.

Roe, K. (2000) "Adolescents media use: A European view", *Journal of Adolescent Health*, *27S*, 15–21.

Rose, M., Rose, G. M. and Blodgett, J. G. (2009) "The effects of interface design and age on children's information processing of Web sites", *Psychology & Marketing*, *26*(1), 1–21.

Ross, J. and Harradine, R. (2004) "I'm not wearing that! Branding and young children", *Journal of Fashion Marketing and Management: An International Journal*, *8*(1), 11–26.

Rossiter, J. R. (1977) "Reliability of a short test measuring children's attitudes towards TV commercials", *Journal of Consumer Research*, 3, 179–184.

Sandhu, N. (2015) "Persuasive advertising and boost in materialism: Impact on quality of life", *IUP Journal of Management Research*, *14*(4), 44–60.

Saaty, T. L. (1980) *The analytic hierarchy process.* New York: McGraw-Hill.

Saaty, T. L. (1994) *Fundamentals of decision making.* Pittsburgh, PA: RWS Publications.

Sachdeva, S. (2009) "Going solo", *Saturday Extra, The Tribune, 25* April.

Schiffman, L. G. (1997) *Consumer behaviour.* New Delhi: Prentice Hall of India (P) Ltd.

Segal, B. and Podoshen, J. S. (2013) "An examination of materialism, conspicuous consumption and gender differences", *International Journal of Consumer Studies*, *37*(2), 189–198.

Selltiz, C. (1962) *Research methods in social relations.* New York: Holt, Rinehard & Winston.

Sener, A. (2011) "Influences of adolescents on family purchasing behaviour: Perceptions of adolescents and parents", *Social Behaviour and Personality*, *39*(6), 747–754.

Shavitt, S., Lowrey, P. M. and Haefner, J. E. (1998) "Public attitudes towards advertising: More favorable than you might think", *Journal of Advertising Research*, *38*(4), 7–10.

Sharma, G. (2008) "Kids take centrestage", *HT Style, The Hindustan Times*, 7 November.

Sheth, J. N. (1974) "A theory of family buying decisions". In J. N. Sheth (ed.), *Models of buyer behaviour* (pp. 17–33). New York: Harper & Row.

Shim, S. (1996) "Adolescent consumer decision-making styles: The consumer socialization perspective", *Psychology & Marketing*, *13*(6), 547–569.

Shim, S. and Gehrt, K. C. (1996) "Hispanic and Native American adolescents: An exploratory study of their approach to shopping", *Journal of Retailing*, *72*(3), 307–324.

Shoham, A. and Dalakas, V. (2003) "Family consumer decision making in Israel: The role of teens and parents", *Journal of Consumer Marketing*, *20*(3), 238–251.

Shoham, A. and Dalakas, V. (2005) "He said, she said they said: Parents and children's assessment of children's influence on family consumption decisions", *Journal of Consumer Marketing*, *22*(3), 152–160.

Singh, B. and Kumar, P. (2003) "Children: An emerging market", *Pragyan, 1*(1), 49–54.

Singh, C. D. and Khamba, J. S. (2015) "AHP analysis of manufacturing competency and strategic success factors", *International Journal in Applied Studies and Production Management, 1*(2), 357–373.

Singh, D. (1998) "Children as consumers", *Indian Management,* (September), 78–81.

Singh, K. and Ahuja, I. S. (2012) "Justification of TQM–TPM implementations in manufacturing organisations using analytical hierarchy process: A decision-making approach under uncertainty", *International Journal of Productivity and Quality Management*, *10*(1), 69–84.

Singh, N., Kwon, I. W. and Pereira, A. (2003) "Cross-cultural consumer socialization: An exploratory study of socialization influences across three ethnic groups", *Psychology & Marketing*, *20*(10), 867–881.

Singh, P. (1992) "Family buying behaviour for TV: An empirical investigation", *Vanijya, 4*(March), 124–133.

Soderqvist, F., Hardell, L., Carlberg, M. and Hansson, K. (2007) "Mild ownership and use of wireless telephones: A population based study of Swedish children aged 7–14 years", *Journal of BMC Public Health, 7*, 105.

Spungin, P. (2004) "Parent power, not pester power", *Young Consumers, 5*(3), 37–40.

Srinivasan, P., Sachitan, R. and Shukla, A. (2006) "The tween economy", *Business Today, 1* January, 53–56.

Stampfl, R. W., Moschis, G. and Lawton, J. T. (1978) "Consumer education and the preschool child", *Journal of Consumer Affairs*, *12*(1), 12–29.

Stokburger-Sauer, N. E. and Teichmann, K. (2013) "Is luxury just a female thing? The role of gender in luxury brand consumption", *Journal of Business Research*, *66*(7), 889–896.

Strasburger, V. C. (2001) "Children and TV advertising: Nowhere to run, nowhere to hide", *Journal of Developmental and Behavioral Pediatrics*, *22*(3), 185–187.

Sun, T. and Wu, G. (2004) "Consumption patterns of Chinese urban and rural consumers", *Journal of Consumer Marketing, 21*(4), 245–253.

Sushil, P. (1994) "Flexible systems methodology", *Systemic Practice and Action Research, 7,* 633–652.

Sutherland, M. and Galloway, J. (1981) "Role of advertising: Persuasion or agenda setting", *Journal of Advertising Research, 21*(5), 25–29.

Sylva, K. (1994) "School influences on children's development", *Journal of Child Psychology and Psychiatry, 35*(1), 135–170.

Teimourpour, B. and Heidarzadeh Hanzaee, K. (2011) "The impact of culture on luxury consumption behaviour among Iranian consumers", *Journal of Islamic Marketing, 2*(3), 309–328.

Tinson, J., Nancarrow, C. and Brace, I. (2008) "Purchase decision making and the increasing significance of family type", *Journal of Consumer Marketing, 25*(1), 45–56.

Ukpore, B. A. (2010) "Secondary school student's attitude towards consumer education", *African Research Review, 4*(2), 322–334.

Valkenburg, P. M. and Buijzen, M. (2005) "Identifying determinants of young children's brand awareness: Television, parents, and peers", *Journal of Applied Developmental Psychology, 26*(4), 456–468.

Van der Voort, T. H. A., Beentjes, J. W. J., Bovill, M., Gaskell, G., Koolstra, C. M., Livingstone, S. and Marseille, N. (1998) "Young people's ownership and uses of new and old forms of media in Britain and the Netherlands", *European Journal of Communication, 13*(4), 457–477.

Vandana and Lenka, U. (2014) "A review on the role of media in increasing materialism among children", *Procedia Social and Behavioral Sciences, 133*(1), 456–464.

Vecchio, R. P. (2000) "Negative emotion in the workplace: Employee jealousy and envy", *International Journal of Stress Management, 7*(3), 161–179.

Verma, K. P. (1982) "Marketing strategies for a consumer durables: The case of domestic refrigerators", *Indian Journal of Commerce, 35*(4).

Ward, S. (1972) "Children's reactions to commercials", *Journal of Advertising Research, 12*(2), 37–45.

Ward, S. (1974) "Consumer socialization", *Journal of Consumer Research, 1*(2), 1–14.

Ward, S. (1977) *Effects of television advertising on consumer socialization.* Cambridge, MA: Marketing Science Institute.

Ward, S. and Wackman, D. (1971) "Family and media influences on adolescent consumer learning", *American Behavioral Scientist, 14*(3), 415–429.

Ward, S. and Wackman, D. B. (1972) "Children's purchase influence attempts and parental yielding", *Journal of Marketing Research, IX,* 316–319.

Watten, R. G., Kleiven, J., Fostervold, K. I., Fauske, H. and Volden, F. (2008) "Gender profiles of internet and mobile phone use among Norwegian adolescents", *Seminar.net – International Journal of Media, Technology and Lifelong Learning, 4*(3).

Weinberger, M. G. and Gulas, C. S. (1992) "The impact of humor in advertising", *Journal of Advertising, 21*(4), 35–59.

Williams, L. A. and Burns, A. C. (2000) "Exploring the dimensionality of children's direct influence attempts", *Advances in Consumer Research, 27*, 64–71.

Williams, L. A. and Veeck, A. (1998) "An exploratory study of children's purchase influence in urban China", *Asia Pacific Advances in Consumer Research, 3*, 13–19.

Wilson, G. and Wood, K. (2004) "The influence of children on parental purchases during supermarket shopping", *International Journal of Consumer Studies, 28*(4), 329–336.

Wimalasire, S. F. (2004) "A cross-national study on children's purchasing behavior and parental response", *Journal of Consumer Marketing, 21*(4), 274–285.

Wu, S. I. (2003) "The relationship between consumer characteristics and attitude toward online shopping", *Marketing Intelligence & Planning, 21*(1), 37–44.

Yadav, R. and Pathak, G. S. (2014) "Environmental awareness and concern among professional students: A study on gender differences", *Social Science International, 30*(1), 15–29.

Yoon, K. (1980) "A reconciliation among discrete compromise situations", *Journal of the Operational Research Society, 38*(3), 277–286.

Young, B. (2005) "The growing consumer", *Young Consumers, 6*(1), 22–29.

Young, B. M., de Bruin, A. and Eagle, A. (2003) "Attitudes of parents toward advertising to children in the UK, Sweden and New Zealand", *Journal of Marketing Management, 19*(3–4), 475–490.

Yu, P. L. (1973) "A class of solutions for group decision problems", *Management Science, 19*(8), 936–946.

Zelrny, M. (1973) "Compromise programming". In J. L. Cochrane and M. Zeleny (eds), *Multiple criteria decision making*. Columbia: University of South Carolina Press.

Zigler, E. and Child, I. L. (1969) "Socialization", *Handbook of Social Psychology, 3*, 450–589.

Index

Page numbers in **bold** denote tables, those in *italics* denote figures.

188   *Index*